Contents

List of Figures

Music and the Young Mind

Enhancing Brain Development and Engaging Learning

MAUREEN HARRIS

Published in partnership with
MENC: The National Association for Music Education

ROWMAN & LITTLEFIELD EDUCATION
Lanham • New York • Toronto • Plymouth, UK

Published in partnership with
MENC: The National Association for Music Education

Published in the United States of America
by Rowman & Littlefield Education
A Division of Rowman & Littlefield Publishers, Inc.
A wholly owned subsidary of The Rowman & Littlefield Publishing Group, Inc.
4501 Forbes Boulevard, Suite 200, Lanham, Maryland 20706
www.rowmaneducation.com

Estover Road
Plymouth PL6 7PY
United Kingdom

British Library Cataloguing in Publication Information Available

Library of Congress Cataloging-in-Publication Data

Harris, Maureen, 1956–
  Music and the young mind : enhancing brain development and engaging learning /
Maureen Harris.
      p. cm.
  "Published in partnership with MENC: The National Association for Music
Education."
  ISBN 978-1-60709-061-8 (cloth : alk. paper) — ISBN 978-1-60709-062-5 (pbk. :
alk. paper) — ISBN 978-1-60709-063-2 (ebook)
  1. Preschool music—Instruction and study. 2. Early childhood education. I. Harris,
Maureen, 1956– II. MENC, the National Association for Music Education (U.S.) III.
Title.
  MT1 .H228 2009
  372.87/049—dc22   2009012202

♾™ The paper used in this publication meets the minimum requirements of
American National Standard for Information Sciences—Permanence of
Paper for Printed Library Materials, ANSI/NISO Z39.48-1992.
Manufactured in the United States of America.

Foreword

Formal study of early childhood music in the United States probably began with the Iowa Child Welfare Research Station preschool laboratory on the University of Iowa campus in the 1920s and 1930s. There research on rhythmic and vocal behaviors of three- to five-year-old children was conducted and published. In the 1940s, researchers conducting the Pillsbury studies at Santa Barbara, California, observed and recorded the creative musical behaviors of children. But it was not until 1969 that preschool music education was identified as a goal by the Music Educators National Conference (now MENC: The National Association for Music Education). In that year, the Goals and Objectives (GO) Project identified thirty-five goals and objectives for improving American music education. One of the goals was to expand music education to include preschool music. Related goals challenged music educators to expand music education research and to build effective relationships with other organizations interested in high-quality education for children.

Events that followed continued to support preschool music education. In 1974, *The School Music Program: Description and Standards* (MENC) described important guidelines for music programs for early childhood. The Ohio State University sponsored two conferences (1977, 1979) dealing with music in early childhood as part of their *Current Issues in Music Education* series, and faculty there were instrumental in establishing the MENC Early Childhood Music Special Research Interest Group (ECM-SRIG) in 1980 to encourage research projects and to disseminate research information to childcare workers and teachers. The Music in Early Childhood Conference held at Brigham Young University in 1984 brought together music educators and preschool educators to further encourage effective relationships between the two populations. And in 1994, the National Standards for Music Education included clear guidelines and standards for prekindergarten music education. These and other efforts created a rich environment for early childhood music education growth.

Research studies, articles, books, and curriculum began to flourish as the twentieth century came to a close. Business entered the preschool music world as programs were organized to train interested adults to provide music education for young children and families. Initiatives such as the U.S. Department of Education's Start the Music Summit in 2000, sponsored by MENC, and the National Association of Childhood Education International (NAEYC) encouraged continuing dialogue between music and early childhood educators and took action to ensure that preschool music education be an important part of the nation's continuing educational efforts.

As we enter the twenty-first century, many methods and models of high-quality early childhood music programs are available for music and early childhood educators. *Music and the Young Mind* provides one more option that is comprehensive and provides ready-to-use guidelines. Maureen Harris has provided a summary of the latest research in child development, music development, brain research, and the biology of music-making. Based on the research, she outlines a curriculum that is workable for both music specialists and early childhood educators. Month-by-month lesson plans and recordings provide easy-to-follow sequential guidelines for teaching music skills and concepts. Exploration of songs and instruments from countries around the world speak to the multicultural climate of the twenty-first century. One of the unique features of *Music and the Young Mind* is the inclusion of Montessori's philosophy and didactic music materials. Harris is exposing the general education profession to materials and processes that have heretofore been available primarily to Montessori teachers. Using MENC's National Standards and NAEYC guidelines, she has created a developmentally appropriate curriculum enriched with Montessori materials, philosophy, and strategies.

In her final chapter, "Tomorrow's World," Harris invites us to consider the impact that the education of young children may have on the future success of society. She reminds us that tomorrow's leaders are today's children, and that it is the early childhood environment that largely determines the characteristics and behaviors children form to meet life's challenges. She discusses the power of music instruction and how it might help promote a generation of responsible citizens. She calls on all of us to "work together globally, to save planet Earth by enriching the creative minds of today's children."

Caregivers at the early childhood level and music educators have much to gain by studying this informative, thought-provoking publication. From specific teaching ideas to situating music education within a global perspective, *Music and the Young Mind* provides something for everyone interested in the music education of children. It is a welcome addition to the world of early childhood music education.

Susan Kenney
Associate Professor of Music Education
Brigham Young University—Salt Lake City

Acknowledgments

Thanks to all whose support and dedication have brought me to where I am today!

Most of all I extend a heartfelt thank-you to Miss Julie Roy and teachers, students, and parents of the Children's House Montessori for their assistance in conducting the research upon which *Music and the Young Mind* was built.

I am especially grateful to the MENC editors Frances Ponick and Linda Brown for answering all of my questions and steering me in the right direction whenever I had a problem.

To trusted and treasured colleagues, Dr. E. Gordon and Dr. C. Taggart, Michigan State University; Dr. R. Upitis and Dr. K. Smithrim, Queens University; and Dr. S. Curtis, Concordia University, whose expertise and insights were invaluable to me. To some of the great masters Bach, Mozart, Beethoven, Verdi, Gershwin, and Porter, whose music offered inspiration during the early hours of the morning.

I am indebted to my wonderful, supportive family—my loving Irish parents who gave me an enriched musical beginning to a journey filled with the love of music; my husband Brian for his continued support and encouragement; my daughter Leah for her musical artistry; and my son Scott for his quiet wisdom.

Finally, to all the children of the world, it is my wish that through the global language of music you find peace! My hopes are for the dreams of the children of tomorrow.

Introduction

Is music part of our being? Does music make us smarter? When should music instruction begin, and how? This book is an attempt to answer these questions while offering educators a valuable insight into and suggestions for the musical education of the young mind.

Plato wrote, "Musical training is a more potent instrument than any other for education" (1883, p. 319). This observation was made during a time when music was at the core of society—a time when music was as commonplace as language, necessary for communication, and mandatory for ritual and other forms of celebration. The twenty-first century is worlds apart from the time of Plato, and yet what makes us unique as human beings remains the same.

How can educators put research into practice and benefit from the wealth of knowledge and research acquired over the centuries on the power of music?

The opening section of this book reviews the most current literature and research on music and brain development and addresses explicit links between music and other domains, in particular mathematics and language.

The second section contains chapters on the therapeutic and biological function of music, from music therapy and its value in reaching the special needs child to the positive ramifications for the gifted child. The healing power of music and children's spiritual well-being are discussed, and the age-old questions about human communication are also addressed, such as, What role does music play in human communication given its existence since the beginning of civilization. Is it the essence of who we are?

Chapters 5 and 6 address sustaining teacher-student relationships and the development of the whole child. This discussion explains the beginning steps in developing a successful music curriculum for young children. It demonstrates how to develop a musical repertoire of songs suitable for the young voice and placed within the correct vocal range. Appropriate percussion instruments for use with young children are discussed with examples of how to hold and use each instrument, followed by music compositions that demonstrate specific instruments of the orchestra.

The multicultural chapter suggests ways that early childhood music settings should be formulated to maximize the benefits of a variety of cultural values and practices. With the current explosion of music available through the Internet, multicultural music is more readily obtainable than ever. A timeline of composers and music from ancient times to the present day is discussed along with descriptions of diverse ethnic music styles from around the world.

Next, in chapter 8, a step-by-step guide to music education for the educator and child includes lesson plans for each basic music concept being studied, with suggested songs (available on the accompanying CDs) and musical activities for demonstration purposes. The lessons are set out in a developmentally appropriate sequence for young children and are formatted in an easy-to-follow manner. This section includes a comprehensive list of recorded music, musical websites, and resource materials to further prepare and assist the educator for working in the classroom. Following and practicing these steps will help build the educator's confidence in her ability to teach music to the young child.

The remaining chapters offer suggestions on implementing the lessons and theories presented, whether in the early childhood classroom or a private setting. The required space, logistics, materials, business plans, safety and insurance concerns, record keeping, and parent issues are briefly addressed. The new or experienced music or nonmusic teacher will benefit from following this research-based, tried-and-tested approach. I would also recommend adding and documenting personal observations over time and sharing these resources with fellow educators.

The finale or coda describes possible new directions in music education for young children. Adhering to the high levels of engagement evident in children's play and creating an environment that is sensitive to the spiritual, cultural, and emotional background of the child are the foundations upon which the musical development of the child can flourish.

As you read this book and gain confidence in teaching music to young children, it is my hope that you will also regard music as a biological human need, an incredible vehicle for enhancing intelligence, and a means of connecting and uniting people around the world.

CHAPTER 1

Brain Research and How Children Learn

What the Experts Say

Research suggests that young children have a tremendous capacity to learn from the moment they are born. These first years of life are crucial to a child's cognitive development. This chapter highlights the most recent research on brain development and the role music plays in the development of the young child.

With the help of new technology, brain researchers are gaining insight into what promotes early development—not only intellectual growth, but healthy social and emotional development as well. In the first years, the young brain rapidly builds the complex networks of brain structure and function necessary for mature thought processes to take place. Early experiences have a decisive impact on the architecture of the brain and the nature and extent of future capacities. While genes influence some of this, positive social interactions and stimulating experiences are crucial. Neurologists and psychologists, with the help of recent research, can now confidently argue that how children develop, learn, and grow depends on the continual interplay between nature and nurture.

In the early twentieth century, in contrast to the opinion of the day (which emphasized what children lacked), Swiss psychologist Jean Piaget proposed that the mind of the child is best described in terms of complex cognitive structures. This sparked the birth of a substantial body of research emphasizing the remarkable abilities of the child and his role as active learner (Gelman & Brown, 1986). Research by Thatcher, Walker, and Giudice (1987) found overall continuous cognitive growth, with examples of growth spurts in specific regions at specific times, thus supporting Piaget's stages of development.

By the end of the sixth month of fetal development, most of the brain cells are in place (Berk, 2004). The brain of the newborn child has about 100 billion neurons (cells that transmit nerve impulses in the human body), most of the neurons it will ever have (Schwartz & Begley, 2002). At birth, the brain is 30 percent of its adult weight, by age two it reaches 70 percent, and by age six it is 90 percent (Begley, 1997).

The interconnections among the brain cells are most important to further growth and development. These neuronal connections multiply through stimulating experiences during a child's early years and are necessary for further development of the neural networks needed in later processing (Olsho, 1984; Trehub, Bull, and Thorpe, 1984). Not all neural development is necessary. In a process called neural pruning, the child's brain begins a process of adjustment between the ages of 7–11 and 9–13 where spatially localized loss of brain tissue of up to 50 percent takes place (Thompson & Nelson, 2001). According to researcher Janet DiPietro (2000), the child's brain begins a process of adjustment that eliminates all unnecessary associations in order to concentrate on the maintenance of those associations that it uses. DiPietro suggests that the brain makes these associations at a very rapid pace in response to the various stimuli in the young child's environment and attests to the theory that the first few years of a child's life are crucial to her future learning development.

Exposure to stimulation, such as sight, sound, touch, taste, and smell lead to growth and development of motor, emotional, behavioral, cognitive, and social functioning (Perry, 2000). Experiments with lab animals at the University of Illinois showed that animals in a stimulating environment developed 25 percent more synapses per nerve cell and 80 percent more blood vessels to nourish each cell (Nash, 1997). In contrast, children raised in an impoverished environment who are not exposed to this sensory stimulation create fewer neuronal connections and miss the opportunity to program the brain for later learning (Hodges, 2000). In fact they will develop a brain that is 20–30 percent smaller than normal for their age. A child reared in a bilingual home can easily learn two languages, whereas the child spoken to in only one language loses the ability to either hear or reproduce certain sounds of different languages. Similarly, a child exposed to only the music of one culture may find it difficult to produce or apprehend the nuances of other music (Patel et al., 2004).

On the other hand, optimal periods of growth are considered as times when it is most easy to learn. Although learning can take place at a later stage, it is more difficult, for example, to learn a second language or musical instrument as an adult. Studies by Flohr, Persellin, and Miller (1996 and 1993) concluded that young children exposed to music or receiving music instruction had the ability to detect pitch variations in both music and language better than those children who had not learned music.

How Do Children Learn?

Olsho (1984) showed that during the early months and years of life, the child's brain expands at a pace never matched in later years. Olsho thus believed early experiences to be crucial to the developing architecture of the young brain.

More recently, Edwin Gordon (2003) has argued that a child who is not exposed to music at a young age is deprived of the optimal time for learning and development. Because neural connections are responsible for all types of intelligence, a child's brain develops to its full potential only through exposure to the necessary enriching experiences in early childhood (Hargreaves & Davis, 2000).

Piaget concluded that the young mind functioned through complex cognitive structures where cognitive development proceeded through certain age-appropriate developmental stages with each based upon very different cognitive schemes. His observation of infants led to the conclusion that their responses to environmental stimulation promoted gradual intellectual development during the first two years. In contrast, Gibson (1969) proposed that learning proceeds rapidly due to the initial availability of environmental stimulation, while Vygotsky (1978) emphasized the social environment and the role support and assistance play in the development of thinking in the young child. Despite the contrasting theories, all would agree that the child is an active learner with the ability to assemble and organize material.

The Effect of Music on Brain Functions

The value of music in the education of the child is the focus of much discussion in education today. Cross-cultural studies continue to confirm that music is universal and very much a part of what it means to be human.

Elliott Eisner (1994), who is particularly known for his contributions to school reform in North America, called for the evaluation of the impact of music programs and discovered positive effects on other aspects of living and learning. Reported benefits of the arts included the development of the imagination (Greene, 1995); greater motivation to learn, increased student creativity, lowered dropout rates, and increased social skills (Catterall, 1998). Researchers also reported that students involved in music exhibited higher academic achievement than students not involved in music (Catterall, 1998; Catterall, Chapleau, & Iwanga, 1999).

According to Eisner, the arts were particularly important for experiencing the joy of creating, developing attention to detail, and learning ways of expressing thoughts, knowledge, and feelings beyond words. He suggested that the arts make distinct contributions to learning and may play a part in students' achievement gains. Some researchers suggest that there are specific cognitive links among some of the arts disciplines and other participants—such as a proposed link between music and mathematics—or that perhaps music offers a way for students to become more motivated to learn. Though researchers have not yet proven what aspect of music education causes particular student achievement, current research evidence clearly identifies the benefits of learning through the arts (Vaughn, 2000; Dewey, 1934; Gardner, 1973).

Sound is the most prenatally usable stimulus, and the human fetus is exposed to many environmental sounds, in addition to the mother's voice, breathing, and movements. The fetal auditory system begins to process sounds between 16 and 20 weeks and reaches adult abilities of development by birth (Lecanuet, 1996). Fetal responses make this development apparent. A baby's preference can be monitored by the intensity in which she sucks a pacifier. Researchers used this method to study babies' preferences for different sounds and discovered that newborns prefer the sound of their mother's voices (DeCasper & Fifer, 1980). Further studies showed that fetuses at 29–37 weeks gestation showed specific behavioral responses to tunes played earlier in pregnancy. Babies studied at 2–4 days of age who had been exposed to a melody repeatedly while their mothers were pregnant, exhibited changes in heart rates and movements when the same melody was presented after birth. In both experiments, behavioral responses were specific to the tune to which they had been exposed (Lecanuet, 1996).

These results indicated that prenatal hearing and the learning and remembering of a melody occurred not only before birth but actually before or at the beginning of the third trimester (Hepper, 1991). The heart rate responding to sound begins at about twenty weeks (Lecanuet, 1996), and a musical slow beat reduces stress while a faster beat increases stress. Classical music played at a rhythm of sixty beats per minute, which is equivalent to that of a resting human heart, has the potential to encourage creative and intellectual development for the unborn child (Verny, 1981).

Anthropologists tell us that humans have always used language and music as modes of expression (Blacking, 1973). A child, regardless of environment or experience, will respond to a sung lullaby. However, because music extends beyond the language of one group of people, it has even more power to touch us. In a rather interesting study on the sound making of animals, Brody (1991) concluded that territoriality, signaling, courtship, and mating served as the motivators for the production of sound rather than humans' desire for aesthetic pleasure. Animals also relied on frequency analysis (D'Amato, 1988) as opposed to the human preference of relative pitch (Trehub, Bull, & Thorpe, 1984), such as the ability to recognize a familiar song regardless of the pitch of the starting note.

While empirical evidence is incomplete and studies have not yet demonstrated the success of prenatal music education, research clearly demonstrates that the first years in a child's life constitute an extremely important time when music can stimulate the development of nerve connections among brain cells for optimal cognitive development.

A study by Whitwell (1997) dealt with the left-brain/right-brain issue and showed that talking about music used the left side of the brain, while creatively producing music used the right side. Hickerson (1983) compared the performance of the left and right hemispheres of the brain through processing tasks of kindergarten students with three different instructional approaches: Montessori, Open Activity-Centered, and Traditional-Conventional. Though there was no statistically significant difference among the instructional approaches, females in all three approaches consistently scored higher on left-brain tasks than males did. Males from all three approaches consistently scored higher on right-brain tasks. The only significant difference was found in the Montessori class; experimental groups from the Open Activity-Centered and Traditional-Conventional approaches scored consistently higher on right-brain tasks than control groups did from the Montessori classes. These results suggest the differences are due more to the influences of the Montessori environment rather than gender.

Music greatly assists making sense of patterns when the development of right-brain activities, such as creativity, artistic expression, and musical intelligence, begins and heightens around age four. This process proves essential to developing life-long thinking skills that lead to enhanced natural development of communication, expression, and cognition (Weinberger, 1998a). More recent research (Finnerty, 1999) suggests that locating the area of musical knowledge in the brain is just not that simple because it is not localized in one specific region. The fact that music experiences are multimodal—involving auditory, visual, memory, emotion, and motor skills—suggests that musical processing uses many areas of the brain. The power of music helps the brain develop, integrates the two hemispheres, and plays a crucial role in the neurological development of the child.

Communication and Language

All cultures have always used music for celebrations and traditions. Music and sound communicate from the very beginning of life. A baby's first cry is a means of communication. Research evidence on music and the baby's brain is very limited; there is still so much to be learned. Thus it is wise to keep an open mind regarding external influences on brain development until neuromusical researchers provide a clearer picture of the child's musical brain development. This should not discount, however, that research has shown that infants in cultures all over the world have innate musical behaviors, and they use music as meaningful communication in their earliest years of development (Weinberger, 1999). Through movement, the very young child will chant a nursery rhyme with a lilt in his voice and an instinctive grouping of words into rhythmic pulses of varying lengths. Rhythm can be felt in virtually all of life experiences, from breathing to walking, and is most naturally expressed in speech.

Edwin Gordon (2003) compares learning music to learning language and stresses the importance of early exposure to both. Consider the infant's first lessons in language. From birth, if not earlier, children are exposed to the sounds of spoken language surrounding them, which they internalize without apprehension. Over time, usually in about nine months, children have the ability to imitate and articulate these sounds of their culture. With much reinforcement, response, and interaction from a caregiver, children slowly learn to transform their sounds into spoken language. It is these words and sentences that children later learn to read and write and eventually perfect through school education.

Gordon (2003) states that this process of development contains four stages—listening, speaking, reading, and writing—that begin at birth and end just after kindergarten. If children do not proceed through these developmental stages, they will not be prepared to benefit from formal language instruction. The same is true of music learning. It is essential that children are sung to as frequently as they are spoken to, and in order for them to absorb the varied sounds of music, they need to hear music frequently. Gordon argues that children who have not developed musical listening, singing, and vocabulary chanting skills later have difficulty relating to and understanding the music of their culture. The first eighteen months are crucial to providing children with the necessary preparation for further music learning. Failure to expose children to music early in life puts them at a disadvantage for later participation in the "making" of music, relegating them to just learning "about" music.

At the approximate age of three years, children begin to achieve lateralization of brain function, which becomes evident as a dominant hand for writing or throwing or a dominant foot for kicking. Experts consider this lateralization to be essential for language development and developing skills for processing information (Galliford, 2006).

The brain's ability to process various forms of information allows the child to communicate. Communication relies on the interaction of the whole brain, and research suggests that speech stimulation is processed in the left hemisphere (Kandel, Schwartz, & Jessell, 2000), while music is processed in the right hemisphere (Rauscher & Zupan, 2000; Rauscher, et al., 1997). Since vocal inflection, speech rhythm, and melodic intonation are processed in the right hemisphere, perhaps this aspect of communication has a stronger connection with music. Evidence shows clearly that the early years are a period when children are biologically predisposed to learning, and consistent external stimulation is necessary throughout this critical period of brain development (Golden, 1994).

Babies are born with brain-mapping capabilities for sound recognition (Kuhl, 2000) and the capacity to learn and articulate the smallest units of language that are known as "phonemes" (Adams, 1990). Children learn the mother tongue by continuous practice recreating phonemes and by hearing and imitating, in the form of language babble, speech, and song modeled by caregivers (Papousek & Papousek, 1981). Although the clarity of speech modeled by the caregiver influences an infant's pattern of articulation (Liu, Kuhl, & Tsao, 2003), neglect or limited practice of verbal interactions can delay language development. This also applies to singing and the child's ability to imitate and match pitch. The nuances that children express in speech and song become evident long before they learn phonics and spelling (Papousek, 1994).

Gromko (2005) explored the relationship between music training and phonemic awareness in young children. The results of the study showed that young children who received four months of music instruction performed significantly better on a test of phoneme-segmentation fluency when compared to the control group. She discovered that those children who sang folk songs accompanied by body percussion and movement to beat, text rhythm, and phrasing were more skilled in hearing a word and responding with its component sounds (phonemes).

Gordon (1997) suggests that just as children learn the foundation of language at home before starting school, they should also learn the foundation of music listening and singing vocabularies. From birth the young child is immersed in the sounds of language and perfects these language skills over time. Reading to the young child with clear enunciation provides opportunities for aural comprehension and exploration of sounds heard. The child begins to speak with babble and through practice and reinforcement eventually forms words and word patterns that lead to sentences. At this very young age, do not expect the child to read and write; just let her explore and learn.

This model of learning language applies to the development of music literacy. Just as children develop an ear for the language surrounding them, they develop an ear for expressive singing and eventually respond musically to what they hear and feel when they are sung to (Feierabend, 1997). Gordon (1997) parallels the stages of music development to the stages of language development that move from experimentation with sound to its imitation and then to its assimilation. At the final stage of music development, the child begins to coordinate singing with breathing and movement, tonal and rhythm skills become accurate, and a sense of beat and a tonal center become present.

Galliford (2006) studied 307 children between the ages of 3 and 5 years to measure whether exposure to varying durations of music and diverse qualities of musical instruction exhibited differences in the development of linguistic and nonlinguistic skills. Galliford assessed the following variables to determine their relative influence on both linguistic and nonlinguistic development: gender, quantity of musical exposure in the first three years of life through either home or school environments, and socioeconomic status of the parents of the participants.

Results indicated that there was a significant association between the total quantity of musical exposure experienced by each participant and the development of linguistic and nonlinguistic skills. Overall, the analysis of the results disclosed the absence of gender differences, and the influence of music on linguistic and nonlinguistic development was independent of socioeconomic status. These latter results are significant due to previous studies indicating a strong correlation between socioeconomic status and educational success (Burt, Holm, & Dodd, 1999; Boudreau & Hedberg 1999) and decreased language abilities in children from lower socioeconomic backgrounds. Another significant correlation was found between the quantity of music exposure and test outcome, indicating that regardless of socioeconomic status, children demonstrated higher linguistic and nonlinguistic abilities based on the consistency and quantity of music exposure.

This study supports earlier research indicating that music stimuli during the formative years of the brain development positively affect the development of cognitive-related abilities (Rauscher & Zupan, 2000; Persellin, 2000). It also supports the unexpected finding that music positively influences the development of linguistic skills in young children.

Roehmann & Wilson (1988) found that Jean Houston of the Foundation for Mind Research believes that children without access to an arts program are actually damaging their brain. They are not being engaged to nonverbal modalities that help them learn skills like reading, writing, and mathematics.

The primary difference between speech and music is the velocity of frequency changes in milliseconds, in which music is slower than speech (Galliford, 2006). The characteristics of music, such as frequency, intensity of rhythm, cadences, and chord progression, compel Galliford to raise the question, "What is the connection between the ear and the brain?" Additional research, however, is needed.

Motor Skills and Movement

Sucking is one of the first mobile acts of an infant, followed by the startled response of arms and legs flung outward from the body. Movement is a survival skill for humans and develops early without instruction or mimicry (for example, blind children learn to walk without being taught). On the other hand, highly specialized and coordinated movement patterns, such as violin playing or tap dancing must be taught and mastered. Outer spatial perception and a high level of rapid spatial processing is needed for ball sports, whereas gymnastics, ballet, swimming, and skating require the opposite and rely upon joint and muscle communication. Children master these skills more readily if instruction begins at an early age (Levine, 2002).

The five forms of motor function are gross motor function, fine motor function, graphomotor function, musical motor function, and oromotor function. Gross motor function uses the large muscle groups necessary for riding a bicycle or playing soccer while the fine motor function controls hand-eye coordination in which visual pathways and fingers coordinate closely, such as using scissors or painting. A graphic artist uses fine motor functions, but the highly specialized graphomotor function is used in writing. Cursive writing, for example, involves the mastery of an unending flow of lengthy visual sequences. Similar to graphomotor function, the oromotor function involves rapid motor sequencing to chew food and to execute all oral communications, from speech to singing (Levine, 2002).

Quite often, the children who have difficulty with speech in preschool also have trouble with writing in the early grades in school. Successful mastering of motor skills boosts a child's self-esteem and provides opportunities to participate in recreational activities in the early school years. Musical motor function uses a wide range of muscular responses while playing musical instruments, dancing, or singing. Exploring musical options to improve motor skills comes in the form of dancing and marching for the development of gross motor functions; playing piano and guitar demands rapid motor sequencing abilities, playing trombone stresses the use of large limb muscles, and playing flute demands more fine motor functions. Without doubt, mastering any of the above highly attuned musical motor functions can do much to bolster the self-esteem of children.

Many school-aged children have difficulty walking to a steady beat and performing simple gross motor skills (Weikart, 1987). These fundamental motor patterns are evident before the age of five and merely stabilized beyond that age (Gilbert, 1979). Hargreaves (1994) suggested that learning occurs through movement and quick emotional associations until a major leap in brain growth takes place in the elementary years. This finding further supports the notion that young children inherently express themselves through music and movement and tactile kinesthetic experiences. Takahashi, director of the Suzuki Talent Education Institute in Matsumoto, Japan, believes that music must be experienced first through awareness of the body, then expressed in the whole body through controlled body movements, and then sung, before being played on any instrument.

Social Skills

Some of childhood's social challenges are (a) seeking friendship, which can be perceived as long-term security against loneliness and self-doubt, or (b) seeking popularity, which consists more of having a positive reputation among a larger group of peers. All of us have been on the receiving end, or witnessed the cruel and thoughtless actions of children toward another. Unfortunately, some children are less skilled than others at succeeding in these areas. The desire or desperation to fit in socially creates many social conflicts and heavily preoccupies the young child. While a substantial amount of social ability is inborn, some can learn to handle the stress better than others (Levine, 2002).

Musical play has many benefits. Children have a natural desire to play and sing, with enjoyment as the only goal. It is a long-held belief that play facilitates growth associated positively with learning and development. The psychologist Brian Sutton-Smith (1997) suggests that additional characteristics of play are that it is variable, it is initiated by the child, participation is voluntary, and rules are set by the players while having fun. Play is improvisational by nature, and completely engages the child. Play also serves as a form of social interaction; social skills, rules, and turn-taking are all learned and practiced through interactive play, while play reinforces expected cultural behaviors (Blacking, 1995). Typically interactive play between an adult and an infant consists of vocalized pitch and volume with varying rhythm that simulates playful exchanges coordinated between the two. These are crucial to the development of close relationships and music has these same characteristics (Trevarthen & Malloch, 2002).

In addition to parallels between music and play, Campbell (1998) discovered that children used music in many ways. Music assists children in forming an identity and maintaining emotional stability and is self-initiated. The creative process is also at work in children's play, as seen in transformed repeated ideas—taking a concept or idea and transforming and repeating it in another area of learning, like the ability to repeat patterns in music and transforming that pattern repetition into language—such as jumping rope and improvising on the initial concept, all of which is quite spontaneous and carried out in the search for novelty (Young, 2003). Whitwell (1997) contends that creative participation in music improves self-image and self-awareness and creates positive attitudes about oneself. This finding is important because "positive" experiences are associated with the development of knowledge, skills, and concepts (Cobb, Yackel, & Wood, 1992).

Concentration

Does baroque music improve concentration? Stein, Hardy, and Totten (1982) studied the effect of music and movement on memorization and retention skills. In the experimental group, students were asked to remember twenty-five words while listening to Handel's *Water Music*. The results of the study showed that those who listened to Handel's music while memorizing scored higher than those who memorized in silence. Further influencing the study was the brain's use of both its right and left hemispheres. George Lozanov's studies on music and memory led to what is known as the Schumann resonance. This refers to the electromagnetic frequency of the brain when it registers 7.5 cycles per second, or the range of meditative thought (Ostrandra & Schroeder, 1979). Ostrandra and Schroeder believed that slowing down the heartbeat and relaxing the body aided concentration and memorization skills. Lozanov (as cited in Ostrandra & Schroeder, 1979) believed that music assisted the body in relaxing while the mind remained alert. His research showed that music of a beat most similar to baroque music had the ability to synchronize the rhythms of the body—heart and brain waves—to the beat of the music. A ten-year longitudinal study conducted by Dr. Norio Owaki (cited in Ostrandra & Schroeder, 1979) showed that music and sound could change brain wave activity.

Music Therapy

Research suggests that music therapy is beneficial in teaching both social and academic skills to young children. Music therapists often work with preschool children and children with Attention Deficit Hyperactivity Disorder (ADHD). Jackson (2003) conducted a survey to ascertain the music therapy methods used for children with an ADHD diagnosis, how effective the music therapist perceived this treatment to be, and the role that music therapy treatment played in relation to other forms of treatment. The results of the survey indicated that music therapists often use a number of music therapy methods that include role-turn playing with percussion instruments, leading rhythmic compositions, and movement to music to treat children with ADHD.

Register (2004) examined the effects of a music therapy program on teaching reading skills and also compared on- and off-task behavior of students during video versus live music conditions. This study confirmed that music increased the on-task behavior of students and supported the need for further investigation regarding the benefits of enrichment programs, particularly programs that incorporated music activities.

Higher-Level Thinking

Higher-level thinking is activated when children encounter challenges with solutions or meanings that are not immediately obvious. There are five areas of higher-level thinking: thinking with concepts, problem solving, critical thinking, thinking with rules, and creative thought. Children deficient in any of these areas will resort to memorizing by rote or imitation and may not be able to engage in in-depth learning (Levine, 2002). Each area of higher-level thinking is highly specialized, and strengths and weaknesses in either area can differ widely from one child to another. Children who can memorize facts extremely well and carry out most procedures by rote, but cannot generalize or use what they learn, have mastered basic skills but not the higher plane of thinking. Fertile higher thinking for all students is the parent and educator's goal and should be nourished from an early age. Each and every one of us thinks in a different way, and these higher-level thinking skills become crucial as children progress through school.

Rauscher et al. (1997) explored the link between music and intelligence in a two-year study with preschoolers. They reported that music training—specifically piano instruction—was far superior to computer instruction on how to use a computer for dramatically enhancing the abstract reasoning skills necessary for learning mathematics and science. Rauscher and Shaw (1998) set out to compare the effects of musical and nonmusical training on intellectual development. The experiment involved seventy-eight three- to four-year-old children of normal intelligence from three preschools in Southern California. Thirty-four of these children received private piano lessons, twenty received private computer instruction, ten received singing lessons, and fourteen in a control group received no special lessons. None had prior music lessons or computer training. Those children who received piano/keyboard training performed 34 percent higher on tests measuring spatial-temporal ability than the others. What Rauscher and Shaw emphasized was the causal relationship between early music training and the development of the neural circuitry that governs spatial intelligence.

Rauscher colleagues (1997) found a connection to the brain linking musical and spatial skills while studying higher brain function. Children who took music lessons scored up to 35 percent higher on spatial tasks, and music lessons improved the spatial-temporal reasoning abilities of four- to six-year-olds. Perhaps listening to specific music enhances spatial-temporal reasoning.

Music students also outperformed nonmusic students on achievement tests in reading and mathematics in a study of medical school applicants. Sixty-six percent of music students who applied to medical school were admitted, the highest percentage of all groups. Students who studied music also scored higher on both the verbal and mathematics portions of the SAT than nonmusic students (Mickela, 1990).

Further research suggested that music should assume a place in the regular school curriculum as it positively affected academic achievement. "Music and the arts were vital to the development and expanse of the human intellect, which in turn resulted in superior academic and career performance" (Oddleifson as cited in Kelstrom, 1998).

A child may use the ability for logical thinking that she developed in music class to solve problems quite unrelated to music. Music profoundly influences the academic life of a child and deserves equal status within the curriculum (Sloboda, 2001). These studies present a compelling argument in favor of the implementation of long-term developmental music programs for all students, not just those students with an obvious aptitude and interest.

The well-known Mozart effect study, which was conducted by Rauscher, Shaw, and Ky (1995), found that students performed better on spatial tasks from the Stanford-Binet Intelligence Test after listening to ten minutes of Mozart's Sonata for Two Pianos in D major. It should be noted a similar study was conducted by Morton, Kershner, and Siegel (1990) from the University of Windsor, Canada, replacing Mozart's sonata with the music of Pink Floyd, and the study produced similar results. Also, several attempts by other researchers to replicate the Mozart effect under similar conditions were not successful (Carstens, Huskins, & Hounshell, 1995). However, what is of interest, with media attention at a height, country-music fan and Governor Zell Miller asked the legislature to spend $105,000 to pay for CDs for distribution to all newborns in the state of Georgia (Kirchner, 1998). It was his intent to expose the newborns to soothing classical music in the hope of boosting brain power. While there is no doubt that listening to classical music was not a negative experience to the newborns, it certainly raises the need for caution and the understanding that research is rarely conclusive.

Reading

The ability to read begins with phonemic awareness and auditory processing, which is the ability to perceive and respond to sound (O'Herron & Siebenaler, 2006). Early in life the young child's brain is wired for imitation and patterning, and the child systematically learns to discriminate between like and unlike pitches, rhythms, and phonemes while developing a sensitivity to the smallest units of sound in language. Listening is the ability to filter, analyze, and respond to sounds (Jensen, 2001), and auditory perception relates both to learning music and learning language. However, not all auditory discrimination skills have equal value when learning to read. Lamb and Gregory (1993) assessed four- and five-year-olds' ability to (a) isolate and manipulate phonemes in words, (b) read, and (c) recognize musical sounds. Students with high phonic awareness scored higher in reading ability as well as pitch discrimination, which is important for recognizing the different qualities of sounds. Music, though, is perceived as patterns, similar to phrases in speech. Technically a musical note is defined as frequency and duration within a musical phrase, somewhat comparable to a phoneme within a word (Sloboda, 1985). Some aspects of sound patterning are shared between the language and musical domains of the brain (Gruhn, Altenmuller, & Babler, 1997; Patel, 1998).

The National Reading Panel (NRP), a research review group, recommends the development of phonemic awareness and prosody (the ability to assemble words into natural speech rhythm with intonation, inflection, and flow) because they are critical prerequisites for learning to read. Educators use music instruction to enhance academic achievement and mental discipline (Upitis & Smithrim, 2001), and evidence suggests that focused listening to music helps some children learn to read, probably by increasing children's awareness of speech sounds, important in "sounding out" words (Butzlaff, 2000). Music, specifically song, constitutes one of the best ways for babies to learn to recognize the tones that add up to spoken language.

The study "Project Zero," conducted by a research group at Harvard University since 1967, reports that while very young children can reproduce specific pitches with considerable accuracy, intervals, and melodic fragments develop much later. By age three, children appear to have a sense of the rhythmic structure of songs and can reproduce fragments of songs. By four years of age, they attempt to reproduce whole songs, although usually without stability of key or tonality, and only at five or six years of age are specific intervals sung correctly (Gardner, 1973). Research by Schlaug (1999) suggests that all children should begin music instruction before they turn seven to obtain optimal brain development.

A study by Hurwitz, Wolff, Bortnick, and Kokas (1975) asked whether music training improved reading performance in first-grade children. The experimental group received Kodály training which used folk songs and emphasized melodic and rhythmic elements. The control group—consisting of children matched in age, IQ, and socioeconomic status at the beginning of the study—received no special treatment. The music instruction was extensive—five days a week for forty minutes each day, for seven months. Students were tested on reading ability at the start of the school year and retested at the end of the year. After training, the music group exhibited significantly higher reading scores than the control group. Music training continued and after an additional year of Kodály training, the experimental group still performed better than the control group. A reading program in New York dramatically improved reading achievement scores by including music and art in the curriculum (New York City Board of Education, 1980). These findings support the view that music education assists in developing the ability to read.

Mathematics

Mickela (1990) conducted a study of 500,000 students in forty-five countries showing that the United States was below average in mathematics. This is significant because a grasp of proportional mathematics and fractions is a prerequisite to mathematics at higher levels, and children who do not master these areas of mathematics cannot understand more advanced mathematical concepts that are critical to higher-order thinking.

I (Harris, 2005a) conducted research studying the differences in mathematics scores between students who received traditional Montessori instruction and students who received music-enriched Montessori instruction. A sample of 200 Montessori students aged three- to five-years-old were selected and randomly placed in one of two groups. The experimental group received a treatment consisting of three half-hour sessions per week in music instruction for six consecutive months. The experimental treatment was an "in-house" music-enriched Montessori program and was sequenced in order to teach concepts relating to pitch, dynamics, duration, timbre, and form as well as skills in moving, playing, listening, singing, and organizing sound. The comparison control group received traditional Montessori instruction based on a three-year program that concentrated on the practical life, and the sensorial, language, mathematical, and cultural (including music) areas of development and did not include a specific music curriculum. The Test of Early Mathematics Ability-3 was used to determine if music instruction had affected students' mathematics test scores. The test covered (a) concepts of relative magnitude, (b) counting skills, (c) calculation skills, (d) knowledge of conventions, and (e) number facts. Results showed that subjects who received music-enriched Montessori instruction had significantly higher mathematics scores.

Rauscher and Shaw (1998) emphasize a causal relationship between early music training and the development of the neural circuitry that governs spatial intelligence. Their studies indicate that music training generates the neural connections used for abstract reasoning, including those necessary for understanding mathematical concepts. Their 1997 study exploring the link between music and intelligence reported that music training, specifically piano instruction, was far superior to computer instruction in dramatically enhancing children's abstract reasoning skills necessary for learning mathematics and science.

Early childhood music provides contexts where creative, conceptual, and logical thinking combine, presenting windows of opportunity for the development and reinforcement of mathematical concepts (Kalmar, 1989). A New York City program called LEAP (Learning through an Expanded Arts Program) uses art and music to teach academic skills. Simple mathematical concepts, such as odd and even, counting, addition, multiplication, sets, and fractions are integrated throughout the musically enriched lessons (Dean & Gross, 1992). As students developed the rhythms for their songs, they began to think in multiples of four. They realized that if they had sixteen beats of music, they had four sets of four beats. Students also grasped the concept of odd and even when the groups were subdivided into smaller units for particular steps or musical rounds (Dean, 1992).

Similar brain processes function to develop a strong sense of musical pitch and the understanding and use of numbers. Pitches in a musical scale and numbers increase from step to step and from lower to higher. The representations, though different, require a similar way of understanding and using information (Gardiner, Fox, Knowles, & Jeffrey, 1996). Music can teach and reinforce basic mathematical concepts otherwise difficult to grasp for some students (Geoghegan & Mitchelmore, 1996).

Mathematics and music were noted for their crossover talents for more than just coincidence. For example, the musical scale is similar to a neat logarithmic progression of frequencies and patterns of notes and patterns of numbers that share similar connections. Music involves ratios, regularity, and patterns, all of which parallel mathematical concepts. Though music is viewed as a separate type of intelligence, high performance in math and music have a significant correlation. Reading music requires an understanding of ratios and proportions. Arithmetic progressions in music correspond to geometric progressions in mathematics; that is, the relation between the two was logarithmic (Marsh, 1999).

Case studies have assessed the academic success of school music students (Milley, Buchen, Oderlund, & Mortatotti, 1983). Rhythm students learned the concept of fractions more easily, and those students who learned rhythm notation scored 100 percent higher on fractions tests. The sixty-seven individual case studies showed that students' achievement in mathematics improved when arts were included in the curriculum. Mickela (as cited in Kelstrom, 1998) also believed that studying music enabled students to learn multiplication tables and mathematics formulas more easily. These findings indicated that music uniquely enhanced higher brain functions required for mathematics, chess, science, and engineering. Because neural connections were responsible for all types of intelligence, a child's brain developed to its full potential only with exposure to the necessary enriching experiences in early childhood (Hargreaves & Davis, 2000).

Creativity

Research predicts early childhood musical experiences and early childhood mathematical experiences can reflect conjoint dimensions (Geoghegan & Mitchelmore, 1996). Learning Through the Arts (LTTA) was initiated in 1994 by the Royal Conservatory of Music, Toronto, Canada, and focuses on teaching core academics through arts-based activities that engage the child (Catterall, 1998). Engagement means that children are wholly involved, physically, emotionally, intellectually, and socially, as Hoffman (2003) describes a science class using LTTA:

> The class is gathered at one end of the gym. Half the kids are walking around in a tight little clump in time to a deliberate beat. . . . Suddenly [the teacher] picks up the pace and the kids follow suit. . . . The marchers speed up and begin to spread out. Turns out this lesson is about energy transfer: The students are water molecules being heated up by a uranium bundle in a nuclear power plant. (When water is heated, each molecule moves more quickly and further apart from the others, hence the change in movement signaled by [the] drum).
>
> Later in the lesson the kids shuffle along the floor, representing electrons moving along power lines. Then they pretend to be atoms joining together and breaking apart, and chant a rap about the pros and cons of various energy sources—all of this to musical accompaniment. (pp. 2–3)

Interviews and surveys with students, parents, teachers, artists, and principals from LTTA schools all indicated that the arts seem to engage children in learning (Upitis, Smithrim, Patteson, & Meban, 2001). Artsvision (an American company developing innovative education projects) recommended the arts as a means of engaging the student and teaching across the curriculum.

Summary

Research supports the theory that music has a positive effect on the development of the brain. Exposing the young child to music earlier in life allows this effect to take place sooner. Musical study at an early age is linked to enlargement later in life in specific areas of the brain that change in response to a stimulus (Campbell, 1997).

This exposure to music must begin early in life, and research suggests that the first eighteen months are crucial to prepare children for further music learning. Failure to expose children to music during these early times deprives them of the optimal time for learning and development (Burton, Horowitz, & Abeles, 1999).

The power of music stretches far beyond its interchange with language, math, and reading. Music uniquely enhances higher brain functions. Music is the soul of creativity, promoting individuality, improved self-esteem, and social skills. Music is the language of feelings with the power to communicate profound emotions. Music is what makes us unique as human beings.

CHAPTER 2

Biology and Music—Tapping the Global Rhythm

Music is indeed universal—it exists in every culture. However, is it a cultural characteristic or a biological/evolutionary development? Do we all beat to a common evolutionary drum? And could music be the universal language—linking minds across cultures and ancestral time? One only needs to walk along the seashore or through a park and listen to the sounds of the environment. Bird and animal sounds fill the air and catch our attention, stimulating us to take action or providing us with comfort. These sounds are similar to sounds humans make, which allow us to identify each other and have many different vocal qualities.

Music, like language, is universal, it occurs in every human culture that we know of and it goes far back into human history. Music may be one of the most ancient and universal forms of human communication. Song is one of the most prominent features in culture, and the human voice has often been identified as the most ancient instrument used in music. Also, the apparent universality of music supports the biological origin of music because behaviors that are closely linked to biology have universality as one of their criteria. It appears that singing developed during evolution and some song structures show similarities to territorial calls, suggesting that singing evolved from loud calls used in a territorial or alarm context. This would then dictate that a similar process took place in the evolution of human singing, and that singing and ultimately music evolved from loud calls of early hominids (Weinberger, 1998b).

"Music is in our genes," says Mark Jude Tramo (2001), a musician, songwriter, and neuroscientist at the Harvard Medical School. "Many researchers are trying to understand melody, harmony, rhythm, and the feelings they produce, at the level of individual brain cells. At this level, there may be a universal set of rules that governs how a limited number of sounds can be combined in an infinite number of ways" (p. 54).

Archaeologists discovered flutes that were made from animal bones by Neanderthals living in Eastern Europe more than 50,000 years ago. Any adaptive behavior in existence for such lengths of time certainly fills the criterion to be a product of evolution. However, there is controversy over this bone flute that was found in Slovenia. One theory is that it is in fact a remnant of a flute, while an opposing theory believes that the bone is simply a gnawed bone, that the holes are coincidentally round and shaped in the proper distance for a flute. The importance of this bone flute is immense since it was found in a Neanderthal dig site and Neanderthals were thought to not have had language because of the shape of their jaws. Naturally, if this is in fact a bone flute, then that would indicate that even if they didn't have language, they had music. Tramo (2001), however, believes that music and dancing preceded language, and no human culture is known that does not have music.

The most likely function of early music was to display and possibly reinforce the unity of a social group toward other groups. In today's world, whenever groups of people define themselves by their music—either by politics, religion, age, ritual, celebration, or function—it is usually through spiritual music, ceremonial music, military music, dance, or sports songs. The origin of social group cohesion may go back to the very beginning of human evolution.

Music has the power to evoke emotion, to express emotion, to make people feel. Some theories suggest that music can have an impact on levels of certain hormones. When music promotes pleasure, it causes the release of endorphins similar to the high long-distance runners experience after running for extended periods of time. Studies show that music causes a biochemical expression such as lowered testosterone levels while listening to favorite music, thus diminishing the heightened testosterone levels necessary for fighting (Lemonick, 2000). Music, it would seem, has the ability to either arouse, when following the rhythmic beat of a call to fight, or soothe and relax the mind and body.

Additional evidence also shows that music does not exist simply for our enjoyment, but rather it affects us in many ways. Some hospitals play soft background music in intensive care units for premature babies. Researchers have found that such music, as well as a nurse's or mother's humming, helps babies gain weight faster and leave the unit earlier than premature babies who don't hear these sounds. On the other end of the age scale, music has been used to calm Alzheimer's patients. At mealtime in nursing homes or hospitals, people suffering from Alzheimer's may be difficult to manage, and fights can occur. It has been demonstrated that the right kind of music reduces confusion and disagreements. Does music lie at the heart—and brain—of what it means to be human? It would seem that everyone is affected by music—the young and old alike.

Music plays a role in social bonding, such as between mothers and their infants, and courting behaviors, such as humans' fascination with love songs that simulate the singing used by birds and chimpanzees to attract mates. As discussed in chapter 1 on brain development, there is evidence that babies can hear music inside their mother's womb. Very young children display musical behaviors and capabilities long before cultural influences begin to shape them (Trehub, 2006). Research on children has shown that they imitate musical phrases and songs and have the ability to compose and perform their own fairly complex songs. These young children have the capabilities of appreciating music and expressing themselves musically (Trehub, 2000).

Of great interest today is the study of cross-cultural recognition of emotion in verbal language and music. Balkwill, Thompson, and Matsunaga (2004) from Queen's University, Canada, conducted a very interesting experiment about the recognition of emotion in Japanese, north Indian, and western music by Japanese listeners. The study randomly assigned the Japanese participants to a music set and these music sets consisted of either Canadian improvised music, Japanese traditional music, or Hindustani ragas music. The objective was for the Japanese participants to rate the style of music assigned to them on scales from "not at all joyful," to "joyful," to "very joyful"; "not at all sad," to "very sad," and so on. The responses were analyzed to assess whether the music that was intended to evoke a specific emotion was recognised as expressing that emotion. The results confirmed that the pieces that were intended to express anger were given the highest ratings on the anger scale, and that was the case for the Canadian, Japanese, and Hindustani music. In general the researcher discovered that for each of the three emotions—anger, joy, and sadness—anger was found to be melodically complex with loud sounds, joy was melodically simple with faster tempos, and sadness was melodically complex with a slow tempo. However, as expected, there was some overlapping, since some of the pieces that were intended to be angry also scored high on the joy scale. Perhaps this is because they share many of the same acoustic cues, such as up-tempo and boisterousness, but differ in terms of complexity. Balkwill and colleagues' research suggests that music is indeed the language of emotion.

As an art form or cultural artefact, music is famous for its emotional power and its ability to affect our mood. Is there any neuroscientific explanation for that? Further neuro-imaging research from Montreal, Canada, supports the fact that music has the ability to alter mood. The researchers took advantage of the fact that some people get chills or shivers down the spine when listening to particular pieces of music. Using only instrumental music to eliminate verbal associations with the text of a song, subjects listened to music as their brains were scanned. The results suggested that they did indeed have chills and shivers as demonstrated by changes in their heart rate. Then the researchers scanned the subjects' brains to monitor brain activity and found some very deep and evolutionarily ancient reward centers of the brain being activated by this purely instrumental music. These areas of the brain are quite significant. They are the areas that are typically activated by biologically significant behavior such as eating or reproducing, and yet they were being activated by this abstract acoustic stimulus with no obvious survival value. The evidence suggests that music has access to some of the most ancient brain structures, tapping into the deepest parts of the brain (Patel, 2003a).

What seems clear is that the building blocks of music are specialized and processed in different parts of the brain, which brings us to one of the big questions in neuroscience today: how does brain circuitry give rise to the mental experiences that we have of the world? Lemonick (2000) assessed children with brain damage who exhibited impairments of certain aspects of music, such as the discrimination of rhythm, while other musical aspects remained intact, such as the discrimination of melody. The study presented science with an opportunity to study the relationship between brain function and complex cognition. Some brain circuits respond specifically to music while also participating in other forms of sound processing. For example, the region of the brain responsible for pitch perception is also involved in determining perfect pitch. Further studies of people with damage to either hemisphere of the brain revealed that stimulation of both sides of the brain resulted in the emergence of music perception.

Why do we feel compelled to move to the beat of music? And why is it that humans are the only species that spontaneously move in response to music? Perhaps the answer lies in the interplay between two brain systems—the auditory system (hearing) and the motor system (movement production) system. Researchers have found activity in brain regions that control movement even when people just listen to music without moving any part of their bodies. Tramo (2001) suggested that just thinking about tapping out a rhythm lights up parts of the motor system in the brain.

The Universal Language—Music?

Music is known as the universal communicator. Whether we understand the language being spoken, music has the ability to cross all cultures, times, and generations and express feeling understood by all. Patel (2003b) of the Neurosciences Institute in San Diego conducted a fascinating study with English and Japanese speakers into how the mother tongue influences the musical ear, and how we group sounds together into larger rhythmic units. Patel explains that when short and simple non-linguistic tone sequences with minimal structures—for example, alternating long and short tones—are played, they are perceived as a repeating segment or a group of some kind. What Patel discovered is that speakers of different languages can hear exactly the same acoustic sequence in very different ways. The evidence suggests that the reason for this was not some inborn difference between Americans and Japanese as listeners, but because particular patterns are reflective of the native language spoken by the two cultures (Patel, 2003b).

Patel believes that music and speech should be regarded as two ends of a "communicative continuum," and not described simply as speech stops here and music begins here. In many cultures, the vocabulary does not include a word for music because music is such an integral part of what it means to be human. However, how important is cultural knowledge for the young child in understanding and finding meaning in music? There appear to be many schools of thought on this topic and no doubt further research is required.

The ethno-musicologists believe that if you were not completely immersed in a culture, or if you didn't grow up in that culture, then you could not appreciate the nuances of the music, and you could not fully grasp the emotional meaning. Catherine Falk (2004), Professor and Dean of the Faculty of Music at the University of Melbourne, suggests that music is utterly entwined with notions of memory, emotion, identity, relationship with place and time, relationship with other human beings, relationship with all living and inanimate objects, relations with the heavens and the gods, and individuals' ways of interpreting their worlds or their cosmologies in their own particular, very culturally specific ways. Mitchell (2007) suggests that people construct the syntax of music in a manner similar to the way they construct themselves socially in their own culturally specific ways. Falk (2004) believes that music is a unique way of knowing the world that has the potential to extend into other ways of knowing the world: visual, linguistic, phonetic, psychological, and mathematical. However, she cautions against misinterpretation and assuming incorrect meanings of music outside the domain of cultural knowledge to people.

However, Patel's (2003b) research study indicates that this is not necessarily the case. The evidence suggests that music can transcend cultural boundaries in order to communicate powerful emotions, and coming from two different worlds or vastly different cultures does not necessarily impact the results. It seems as though music that is intended to communicate emotion, does so universally, and every culture on the planet has a form of communication that could be referred to as musical.

From a psychological perspective, it would seem that music is a universal language since it is relatively easy to blend musics of all cultures (Mitchell, 2007). A group of musicians from different cultures all over the world, who cannot communicate through language, can quite simply pick up from where one leaves off, they can blend, they can intertwine, they can improvise, and they can communicate through music. Music has the unique ability to communicate across cultures.

From the neuroscience perspective, Patel is quite confident that music is a human universal; however, he believes that calling it a language is problematic because it is different from language in so many important ways. We should think of music as a communication system that has deep and important connections to language and that exploring those connections can teach us a lot about music, about language and about the brain itself.

Spirituality and Music

"Music and song were intimate parts of the rites and ceremonies in which the meaning of group life was consummated" (Dewey, 1980, p. 7).

Throughout the history of civilization music has been an integral part of life with a special place in spiritual and religious celebrations. Music making is connected to the earth and the humans who inhabit it. Musical instruments of varying types, tone colors associated with the timbre of the human voice, and the worldly acoustics in which these sounds are made (such as the echo of a cave), all remind us of our spiritual connection with nature. Children are especially receptive and sensitive both to the wonders of musical exploration through handmade instruments from natural materials and to the possibility of creating music and sound with one's own body. The incredible vocal range of a baby's voice encourages endless improvised musical conversations with the environment.

Even with the youngest of children, exploring the musical spiritual dimension is more easily experienced through movement and dance, because children will flow with the music the more their feelings are engaged. Insofar as the physical component of the musical experience is vital for the child, so too is the aural experience. For many, the exploration of musical instruments made from natural materials is a holistic experience. The reverence associated with the tree from which the wooden musical instrument was carved is reestablished each time the instrument is played (Fisher, 2002). Setting the scene for free-flowing imaginative creativity can contribute to the spiritual dimension of the experience. The many therapeutic possibilities of music offer such powerful experiences that they may be described as divine. Experiencing this spiritual dimension can be accomplished through various music-making activities and the right balance between what is experienced and those who experience it. This spiritual awakening within the musical experience is often linked to cultural areas such as ethics, identity, personal and social development, particular cultural traditions, and the feeling of being connected to something beyond and outside oneself (Boyce-Tillman, 2007).

Life without Music

What if life did not include music? Imagine a day in the life of a twenty-first-century child without any music. Waking up in the morning is not induced by an alarm clock or birds whistling, and the morning shower takes place in silence. Once arriving at school the national anthem isn't sung, and the sports games throughout the day are absent any form of music or chanting. School musicals no longer exist and those budding figure skaters and dancers are moving to some inner rhythm desperately in need of a steady beat. Evenings are no longer filled with teenagers listening to the latest music either on their TVs or MP3 players, and the baby is not sung to sleep by a parent. Celebrations around the world are devoid of music, and the father of the bride does not offer his hand to her for the first dance of the evening. Memories of days past are no longer triggered by a familiar musical tune and the universal sounds of planets in motion are gone.

Research by Roehmann and Wilson (1988) supports the theory that music has a positive effect on the development of the brain, and the earlier in life the young child is exposed to music, the sooner this effect begins to take place. Jean Houston (as cited in Roehmann & Wilson) of the Foundation for Mind Research agrees and suggests that children without access to music are actually damaging their brain. They are not being engaged in nonverbal modalities that help them learn skills like reading, writing, and mathematics.

We do not need research to show us that music plays a big part in everyone's life. In the words of the German philosopher Friedrich Nietzsche (1888), "Without music, life would be a mistake."

Does music lie at the heart—and brain—of what it means to be human? The question of the origins of music is without doubt of great interest and is in need of further research as we have only just begun to address the mysteries of music and the human psyche.

CHAPTER 3

Healing

Music has been used in healing for thousands of years. From ancient times and across all cultures, music has been used for emotional expression, communication, religious celebrations, grieving rituals, and entertainment. Ancient Greek philosophers believed that music could heal both the body and the soul, while Native Americans used singing and chanting as part of their healing rituals. The ability to appreciate and respond to music is an inborn quality in human beings.

Music therapy is receiving increasing recognition as a vital part of the health care system and is an appropriate and effective intervention for a wide range of physical, mental, social, and emotional needs. The use of music therapy is also growing rapidly, as evidenced by the increased numbers of participants attending worldwide conferences and the increased numbers of music therapy students at the undergraduate and postgraduate levels of education. Leslie Bunt (1994), a professor of music therapy at the University of West England, describes music therapy as the use of sounds and music within an evolving relationship between the client and the music therapist to support physical, mental, social, emotional, and spiritual well-being. It can also be used to improve physical, psychological, cognitive, and social functioning.

Research studying music therapy intervention includes the amelioration of the impact of abuse such as childhood sexual abuse (La Fontaine, 1990); improved rehabilitation from severe traumatic brain surgery (Glassman, 1991); help for psychiatric disorders (Ficken, 1976); help for families of sexually abused children (Mrazek & Kempe, 1981); survival of premature babies (Nocker-Ribaupierre, 1999); assisting children with eating disorders (Robarts & Sloboda, 1994); helping children deal with traumatic experiences linked to early abandonment, violence, and war (Sutton, 2002); and helping refugee children and those living in multicultural contexts in inner cities (Clough, 2004). For people who find verbal communication an inadequate form of self-expression, music therapy offers a safe, secure space for the release of feelings. It is the special relationship involving the therapist, the music, and the patient that facilitates a desire to express emotions and begin the healing process.

Through whatever form the therapy takes, the therapist aims to facilitate positive changes in behavior and emotional well-being. He also tries to help the client develop an increased sense of self-awareness, and thereby to enhance her quality of life. The therapist adapts the music and style of approach to serve a specific client's needs and the process may take place in individual or group music therapy sessions. The music played covers a wide range of styles in order to complement the individual needs of each client. Much of the music is improvised, thus enhancing the individual nature of each relationship.

History

The more formal approach to music therapy in the United States began in World War II when Veterans Administration hospitals began to use music—instrumental as well as vocal—to help treat soldiers suffering from shell shock. For the first time in history, the U.S. military officially recognized music as an agent capable of helping mentally and physically wounded soldiers and created the music portion of the military's Reconditioning Program (U.S. War Department, 1945). The authorities realized that music helped boost the morale of homesick soldiers and authorized music as a morale-builder and a "drive into battle."

The surgeon general conducted a six-month survey studying the musical tastes of America's war casualties (U.S. War Department, 1945). The survey showed that music could be employed in several effective ways, such as for exercise routines, postoperative exercises for orthopedic or lung cases, educational activities, resocialization, and aiding neuropsychiatric treatment. The War Department's Technical Bulletin 187 provided instructions on the implementation of various music opportunities offered to patients, pointing out the healing powers of music and its ability to bring groups together, release emotions, and create a spirit of fellowship (Green, 1947; Simon, 1945). In neuropsychiatric treatment, music was seen to influence the mood of the patients by evoking pleasant memories of past experiences. The main objective of active participation with music was to aid in the social readjustment of the patient, to boost morale, and to provide occupational therapy. In passive participation, the goal was to assist in the patient's social and mental readjustment, and to stimulate physiological and psychological responses (McKay, 1945). The activities outlined in the technical bulletin were carried out in the 122 Veterans Administration hospitals and, by late 1945, 44 of them had full-time music specialists who worked closely with medical personnel (Green, 1948, 1950).

At the request of the representatives from the Surgeon General's Office and Walter Reed General Hospital, Frances Paperte, an accomplished vocalist, conducted an incredible 3.5-year research study to determine if music presented according to a specific plan could aid in the recovery of military personnel with mental and emotional disorders (Kaempffert, 1944). The musical treatment sessions were divided into three sections: (a) music playing to create basic rapport between patient and musician (mood-determination), (b) patients talking to the musicians, if desired, and (c) patients participating in the sessions. Medical and musical records were kept on all sessions and on all patients. The results positively demonstrated the healing effect of music, from providing the patient with an opportunity to express emotions rather than submerging them deeply into the subconscious, to promoting relaxation and building of self-confidence, to increasing socialization with others with mutual interests. In summary, the research clearly demonstrated that participation in music assisted in removing the feeling of inadequacy, which is at the core of the neurotic patient (Gilman & Paperte, 1952).

The benefits gained from the music therapy were as varied as the soldiers were. For example, music helped convey feeling without the use of words. For those whose difficulties were mainly emotional, music therapy provided a safe setting where "difficult" or repressed feelings were expressed and contained. By offering support and acceptance, the therapist helped the soldiers to work toward emotional release and self-acceptance.

More Recent Studies

Christian Pross (2001) founded a torture therapy centre in 1992 in a Berlin hospital for victims of torture to help them shake off their traumatized past. Most of the patients here are political refugees seeking asylum, and trauma is always at the back of their minds and can be easily triggered. For example, keys jangling or dogs barking can bring back memories of a prison camp. Music therapy helps drown out those memories and replace them with new memories. Pross believes that music can reach deep into the human soul. He has witnessed clinically depressed patients who could not speak suddenly play a simple instrument with gusto.

It is a widely held belief that music has a beneficial effect on the spiritual and emotional aspects of healing and, for much of the twentieth century, medical policies and practices have been driven by science- and technology-based diagnoses and treatments. However, the twenty-first century brings with it the interest of the medical profession in the anxiety-reducing qualities of music, in particular in the treatment of acute pain. Scientific studies have shown the value of music therapy on the body, mind, and spirit of children and adults. Some studies have suggested that, when used with pain-relieving drugs, music may help decrease the overall intensity of the patient's experience of pain (Curtis, 1986; Tse, Chan, & Benzie, 2005). Doctors in Stockport, England, have been able to avoid the need for psychiatric treatment for anxious or depressed patients in hospital by offering "arts on prescription," which includes weekly sessions of painting, creative writing, drama, and music (as cited in Rorke, 1996).

Rather than using music as a potential distraction while the patient quietly listens, what are the effects of music when the patient is participating in activities connected with the music? Such a study was conducted by Laura Noguchi (2006) to determine if a focus-of-attention activity involving music would affect levels of distress and perceptions of pain in pediatric patients receiving injections (six children, four to six years old). The children heard a musical story or a spoken story or received standard care/control. Those children listening to the story also pointed at corresponding pictures throughout the injection process.

The results of the study indicated that the children assigned to the music activity tended to show the least amount of distress when compared to the other children; however, the differences were not found to be significant. The researcher suggests that this may be due to the small sample size (six children) and that a larger group may have projected a more readily detected difference. Given that adult avoidance of medical treatment has been associated with unpleasant medical experiences as a child (Megel, Houser, & Gleaves, 1998), this area of study is most certainly deserving of further research and attention.

CHAPTER 4

Gifted Children

Children with special needs cover the spectrum of ability from challenged to gifted, and each extreme warrants consideration when the child is immersed in an education system designed for the masses. In the previous chapter, I addressed the needs of children with various challenges. I would now like to discuss the equally demanding and challenging needs of the gifted child.

In many cases the exceptional child's needs are met by extracurricular activities initiated and perhaps funded by the parent or caregiver. This raises the question of the exceptional child living in a disadvantaged environment. What can be done to ensure that child develops to his fullest potential?

Throughout history there have been many gifted people in a variety of fields from Albert Einstein (physics) to Leonardo da Vinci (art) and from Baryshnikov (ballet) to Tiger Woods (golf). However, in the field of music, the greatest gifted *child* prodigy was Wolfgang Amadeus Mozart, whose acute sense of listening and sensitivity to sound, pitch, and the overall properties of music were recognizable from birth. Mozart spent considerable time playing the piano and composing music. His father spent incredibly long hours each day at the piano teaching his three-year-old son, as did Ludwig van Beethoven's father. How many child prodigies might we discover today if the environment were similar? More recently, researchers have found that during the early stages of music instruction, children who are provided with parental support and encouragement that emphasize intrinsic rewards tend to persist in their music learning. Such children possess an underlying motivation with intense concentration and passion. Passion provides a desire, a need, or a longing that persists long after discipline or motivation pass. In contrast, the opposite is apparent—children from unsupportive families tend to give up playing at an earlier age (Sloboda & Howe, 1991).

Other influencing factors in the gifted child's development are the educators who assist the parents. Research by Sloboda and Howe (1991) indicates that the most influential educators had a personal warmth, made lessons fun, and showed a fondness for the young student. According to Solomon (1995), Mozart's father could inspire and nurture his students' talents by instilling a commitment to excellence and a sense of unlimited devotion. The impact of teachers and parents on the overall development of the gifted child is quite significant and is crucial to sustaining involvement (McPherson, 2005).

What then can caregivers and educators do to assist the gifted child along the path to her fullest potential? Research indicates that the caregiver's perceptions of the young child's giftedness are usually accurate and are based upon behaviors observed between the child and her peers. However, caregivers may not have confidence in these perceptions. Levine (2002) believes that all children possess gifts or notable strengths. However, he dislikes labeling children "gifted" as if "they are among the lucky few who possess super-neurodevelopmental profiles" (p. 262). He goes on to say, "There is no such thing as a perfect mind. Therefore, every gifted child has some discrete areas of weakness that could cause problems someday. Furthermore, every child I've ever met has had at least one area of potential or actual giftedness as part of his or her neurodevelopmental profile" (p. 262).

Assessment

The most immediate problem is deciphering whether a child is gifted and to what degree. For the most part, the accumulated body of research in the twentieth century has dealt with assessing those children with learning difficulties (Elliott, Argulewicz, & Turco, 1986). The lack of standardization in this area of assessment simply adds to the problem. Assessment of the young child's intellectual giftedness tends to be somewhat unreliable, and scores can be altered by individual insecurities during the testing. However, there are benefits to assessment that provide information regarding appropriate stimulating environments for the child. For example, an intellectually gifted child may benefit from early entrance to preschool or an enriched curriculum designed specifically for his needs. In many cases, children who demonstrate giftedness in one area of development may show signs of weakness in other areas, and testing offers the means to assist the child in practicing these skills. Most important, testing offers a baseline score that may be critical in monitoring the child's intellectual growth and progress over time.

There are two individually administered IQ tests that are appropriate for testing preschool gifted children—the Wechsler Preschool and Primary Scale of Intelligence Revised (WPPSI-R) and the Stanford-Binet Intelligence Scale, Form L-M. Both are mainly verbal tests, with the Stanford-Binet offering a more extensive scale for the very gifted child. For the very young child who is already reading and doing math calculations, it is also advisable to conduct an achievement test orally in a one-on-one setting to attain the most accurate results. Scores become even more reliable when tested around first grade. Once the child is of school age, testing takes place either privately with a private psychologist or by the school psychologist. The intelligence tests of choice are the Wechsler Intelligence Scales, which include a preschool test, a school-age test, and an adolescent/adult test. While these tests are helpful for identifying strengths and weaknesses, they are not necessarily helpful to the gifted child whose score may exceed the limit of 155.

The work of Francoys Gagne (2003) is based on standards used around the world in education and distinguishes between giftedness and talent. He describes talent as a demonstration of superior skills or competency following specific training in a field, such as perhaps music. He defines giftedness as an above average natural predisposition to achieve, and this aptitude is enhanced by a stimulating environment. The environment in conjunction with accumulated practice over a period of approximately 10–15 years spurs the developmental process (Sloboda & Davidson, 1996; Winner, 1996a, b).

Using behavioral rating scales to identify gifted children from majority and minority groups is beneficial for planning programs suitable to these children. One such scale is the Scales for Rating the Behavioral Characteristics of Superior Students (SRBCSS) (Renzulli, 1986). A study by Terman and Oden (1947) revealed that the home environment played a crucial role in the potential IQ scores of gifted children. Approximately one-third of children identified as gifted in the study were children of professional people and about a half were children of persons in business occupations. Therefore, IQ scores reflect educational opportunities of the test takers, a result which suggests that a rich environment causes an increase in IQ scores (Taylor, Hinton, & Wilson, 1995; Tyler, Rafferty, & Tyler, 1962).

Helping the Gifted Child

An enriched, stimulating environment is a necessary tool in assisting the gifted child's development. Shin'ichi Suzuki (1983) based his Japanese Suzuki education system on the belief that all children are musical and can develop musically when exposed to the best possible environment. He makes the comparison to the young child learning to speak his native tongue. It is Suzuki's belief that it is the child's environment that provides him with the high-quality example and opportunity to repeatedly practice under close interactive supervision with the responding adult. Both child and caregiver engage in daily conversations with each other until eventually both are communicating, and the child learns to perfect his language through interaction with the caregiver. Suzuki proposes that music can be learned in a similar manner, through repeated nurturing on the part of the caregiver.

CAREGIVER

When selecting a caregiver or preschool for the young child, communication and consistency between home and school are vital for sharing in the child's developmental milestones, and a daily journal exchange can facilitate this communication. In general, the gifted child may express a thirst for academic learning, and the staff's recognition of his giftedness, individual differences, and needs will promote an environment that values the unique creative and learning abilities of the child. Realistically, no matter how excellent the caregiver or school, the needs of the gifted child may not be fulfilled. Many gifted children start school as highly engaged learners and rapidly become disengaged, encountering serious difficulties as they become bored when their knowledge surpasses that of the teacher. When selecting schools, parents will need both persistence and realistic standards. Continued open communication and creative problem solving between parent, child, caregivers, and educators will influence decision making in a more concrete way. Sadly, due to lack of funding and teacher awareness, many of the specific needs of gifted children can only be met outside school, and outside opportunities are less accessible to children in lower socioeconomic environments. This is a shameful waste of a wonderful human resource (Clark & Akerman, 2006).

AT HOME

At home, parents who are the primary caregivers can enhance their child's learning by encouraging exploration, a love of reading, and an appreciation for culture, the arts, the environment, and the world community, just to mention a few. The initial stages of a child's musical development take place at home with the parent or caregiver. A piano or guitar played by an amateur musician-parent becomes the basis for many sing-alongs and play-alongs. Songs aid in language development and are the first building blocks of a developmentally appropriate music curriculum, while musical stories (without visuals) encourage children's listening skills. The constant interactive singing and talking between child and caregiver develop in a manner very similar to language development and are improvisatory in style, with tonal development mimicking the speech patterns of the caregiver. Dancing to music facilitates the child's coordination and love of music while encouraging a less inhibited family unit.

An important aspect of the child's learning is the inclusion of opportunities for social interaction. When a child is interacting with others, he learns skills that are crucial to further peer relations and teamwork. Musical games provide many avenues for exploration and practice in the art of people skills and offer the added benefit of providing practice in problem-solving skills. Of further importance is motor development, and play is an ideal way to fine-tune gross and fine motor muscle groups.

AT SCHOOL

Education for gifted students is focused on matching curriculum to advanced ability using a curriculum based on the unique characteristics and individual learning needs of the gifted learner. What are the needs of the gifted child and how can the classroom teacher provide these children every opportunity for learning? Depending on the child's particular area of exceptionality, the teacher needs to pull from her "bag of tricks" activities that are stimulating and interesting to the child, without disrupting the classroom routine for the other children. The extensive range of learning requirements for gifted children presents quite a challenge for the classroom teacher.

Learning Requirements

Unusual retentiveness.   The child presenting unusual retentiveness benefits from exposure to a wide range of topics and vast quantities of information. The segment on Prokofiev's *Peter and the Wolf* in chapter 9 enables this child to present to the class pictures of the instruments representing the characters in the musical story and to elaborate upon how these instruments are made, how they compare to each other by sound produced and materials used. These children enjoy sharing their extensive knowledge with their peers.

Advanced comprehension.   Within each lesson plan in chapter 9, there are tools to elaborate and offer access to a more challenging curriculum. For example, during the rhythm and time signature component, the class concentrates on feeling the pulse of the music either through clapping, beating a drum, or stepping, etc. Providing learning activities of appropriate level and pace, such as encouraging this child to clap the rhythm of the music against the steady beat of his peers, enhances advanced learning.

High verbal skills.   Mozart and the Young Mind (MYM) is based upon a repertoire of songs that facilitate the learning of basic musical concepts. Learning the words to these songs may take some time for young children, and providing the highly verbally skilled child with the opportunity to lead the group in song or discuss the meaning of the song adds further opportunities for in-depth discussions.

Flexibility of thought processes.   Gifted children find music class to be the ideal venue for using imagination, imagery, and spatial abilities. Moving to music with the use of scarves to express a story line, such as the biblical fable "The Lion and the Mouse," or in response to how the music "feels" in the music of the American Gershwin—as opposed to the Japanese song "Sakura" or the Norwegian Grieg's "Hall of the Mountain King"—promotes problem solving and creative thinking.

Independent learning.   Provisions for self-direction and development of independence for these children is clearly active during mapping exercises. Each child is encouraged to listen to a song sung by the teacher such as "Row, Row, Row Your

Boat" and draw the interpreted phrasing individually with a marker on bristol-board. There is no wrong or right answer, as the song is experienced, expressed, and represented in the drawing. Each child is actively involved in learning while sharing his work with the other children involved in this independent learning task.

Holistic thinking and emotional sensitivity. Small-group activities and an integrated approach to the curriculum work best with these children, such as working in partners during the "Clap, Clap, Clap" song or "Hello, Hello." The children interact with each other by holding hands, shaking hands, or waving good bye to their special partner. Rowing the boat in "Row, Row, Row Your Boat" is demonstrated by two children sitting and facing each other, holding hands, and rocking in the same direction to the beat of the music. These children enjoy the interaction with their special friend and holding hands, and they need to be sensitive to the partners' needs and responses to the song.

Creative Thinking

Four of the classic childhood creative abilities as suggested by Guilford (1968) and Torrance and Safter (1990) are listed as follows: Fluency, Flexibility, Originality, and Elaboration.

Fluency is the ability to produce many ideas in response to an open-ended problem or question. The ideas may be verbal or nonverbal (e.g., mathematical or musical). A good fluency exercise is rhythm mirroring. Apart from helping with mathematical development, this activity reinforces the child's sense of rhythm. Using a pair of rhythm sticks for each child, and having established rhythm patterns with a clapped response, rhythm patterns can now be increased to two or three varied speeds faster or slower to create interest. Asking students to eliminate—such as minify, condense, lower, shorten, lighten, omit, split up—or change pace—such as change schedule, reverse, transpose, make opposite, reverse roles, turn upside down—adds further interest for the gifted child.

Flexibility is the ability to take different approaches to a problem and think of ideas in different categories, or view a situation from several perspectives, such as introducing playing an instrument to complement singing or to make a familiar story more familiar. Using instruments promotes hand-eye coordination, rhythm development, and a sense of sharing. Of further interest to the gifted child is "musical ice skating," which aids in physical development. Choose gentle classical music and provide a pair of party plates to each child. Ask students to place the plates on the floor and to stand on them. Play the music and encourage the children to ice skate by demonstrating how you slide one foot and then the other as if ice skating on plates. Combine ideas, uses, and purposes by moving slow or fast, forward or backward, and turning, as well as balancing on one foot. The swishing sound created by the friction between the plates and the floor adds an extra rhythmic dimension to the activity. Asking the gifted child to trace the shapes of letters, or numbers, or geometric shapes with his feet continues to create interest and challenges.

Originality is a uniqueness or nonconformity. Knowledge and understanding of the diverse world in which we live may be introduced through displaying musical instruments from different cultures—wooden instruments are ideal because they produce a hollow, low-pitched sound, which is not as piercing as other high-pitched instruments and won't disturb others who are working. To create further interest, substitute, simplify, subtract, or use other materials, other approaches, other children. Adapt other parts, motion, color, sounds, function, and textures, while magnifying, modifying, and minimizing, i.e., make the concept bigger, smaller, lower, higher, or add time or sound, exaggerate shape, make stronger or weaker beats.

Elaboration is the important ability to add details to a given idea: developing, embellishing, and implementing the idea. Activities such as providing a music shelf to which the children have access, and using creative stories for group activities to enrich the gifted child's vocabulary and encourage creativity with language also assist in memory retrieval. Listening to Benjamin Britten's "Young Person's Guide to the Orchestra" sparks further improvisation with instruments, such as those made with different materials, for example, empty paper towel holders filled with beans or rice, bowls covered with plastic or coffee cans with lids for drums, and pan lids for cymbals. The gifted child can be encouraged to experiment with transposition by reproducing simple tunes in varying keys and developing the ability to transpose.

The use of real-life activities encourages original thinking and independent learning, while addressing the issues of values and feelings. For example, spending a day on a farm is a wonderful exploration area for urban and suburban children, while visiting the city with its many art museums, parks, conservatories, museums of natural history, aquariums, observatories, nature centers, and concert halls provides endless learning opportunities for all. Not to mention bringing history alive with a visit to a senior citizens home or spending an afternoon with great-grandparents.

The bottom line is that all children benefit from and deserve enrichment activities and experiences. Bright children benefit from and deserve acceleration. But gifted children may need a completely different learning environment, or mentorships, or rapid acceleration, or all of the above. The key is a truly individualized education, based entirely on the needs and abilities of the child.

experiences are studied, learned, practiced, and then acted out. Song-experience-games create real-life situations for children. The fun of learning each song-experience-game and the repeated practice of the song and game invite and motivate the child to learn with ease (Richards, 1978).

KINDERMUSIK

In 1960, a group of music educators in West Germany developed Musikalische Fruherzienhung, music for young children. The program is designed to help children experience the joy of learning music before beginning formal music instruction. In the 1970s, due to growing popularity, the program was translated and adapted for American children and renamed Kindermusik. In a Kindermusik class, educators lead a group of parents and their children through various activities, using music and movement. Parents learn more about their child's unique developmental process, and the shared learning experience creates a unique bond as the child associates learning with fun and musical play. The Kindermusik curriculum nurtures the whole child beginning with the newborn through age 7. Every lesson moves at the child's pace, pausing to engage his interests.

Kindermusik's foundation of learning provides scientific explanations as to how Kindermusik enhances the natural growth systems of the young mind and body. The Kindermusik teaching objectives are for each student to develop the ability to express what is heard securely, effectively, and knowledgeably through movement before transferring those physical sensations into other forms of musical expression. The Kindermusik method claims that movement and dance activities improve coordination and balance; one-on-one parent and child interaction nurtures self-esteem; music-making and music-listening activities develop self-discipline, as well as critical and creative thinking skills (Kindermusik Foundations of Learning, 2001). The Kindermusik primary goal is to stimulate development in every part of a child's brain through music.

KODÁLY METHOD (ZOLTÁN KODÁLY, 1882–1967)

The Kodály method of music instruction evolved in the Hungarian schools under the inspiration and guidance of Kodály. The goals, philosophy, and principles were Kodály's; however, the pedagogy was not. Solfa was invented in Italy and tonic solfa came from England; rhythm syllables were the invention of Cheve in France and many of the solfa techniques employed were taken from the work of Jaques-Dalcroze; hand-singing was adapted from John Curwen's approach in England (Choksy, 1974); and the teaching process was basically Pestalozzian (Choksy, Abramson, Gillespie, & Woods, 1986). What was unique about Kodály's method was the way in which these previously separate techniques were combined into one unified approach. Kodály based it upon a sequential system of sight singing that leads into the understanding of musical notation. Kodály's basic aim was to teach children to read and write music through singing (Raebeck & Wheeler, 1972).

The principal objectives of Kodály musical training are that, through singing, every student should have the opportunity to become musically literate (in the sense of being able to see a score and imagine the sounds or to hear sounds and imagine the score) and to know and love his or her own folk music heritage and the great art music of the world (Choksy, Abramson, Gillespie, & Woods, 1986). The Kodály Method involves using the instrument that is most accessible to everyone, the human voice. Singing forms the foundation for musical knowledge, artistic sensibility, and social connection (Smee, 2004). The Kodály primary goal is to produce universal musical literacy.

MUSIC LEARNING THEORY (EDWIN GORDON)

The developmentally appropriate music series Jump Right In is based on *A Music Learning Theory for Newborn and Young Children* (Gordon, 2003) and years of practical and experimental research. It is designed to assist teachers, parents, and caregivers of newborns and young children in the development of basic music skills, such as singing, rhythm chanting, and moving, with an emphasis on individual differences between children. Suggested activities guide the child through developmental music stages with corresponding tonal or rhythm patterns. Also, movement activities are encouraged to give children the opportunity to teach themselves how to coordinate their breathing with tonal, rhythm, and movement responses (Gordon, et al., 1998). All of this is accomplished through informal guidance that is based on and operates in consequence to the natural sequential activities and responses of the child.

The primary goal of Music Learning Theory is to approach music education as one would approach language learning right from birth. Through consistent exposure to and reinforcement of musical concepts, the child learns to move through stages of musical development that will provide him with the basic knowledge to study music at school (similar to how the parent assists the child with language development in preparation to starting school).

MUSIC FOR YOUNG CHILDREN (FRANCES BALODIS, 1949–)

Music for Young Children (MYC) was created in 1980 by education specialist Frances Balodis. Her intent was to create a comprehensive and fun beginning music program for both parent and child in a small group setting. The program uses early childhood development techniques to provide music instruction in a positive and comprehensive way. The parent and child are taught as a team while having fun together learning keyboard, singing, rhythm ear training, sight-reading, theory, history, and composing (Nye, 1983). Games and activities are used to reinforce the lesson's objectives using the child's visual, auditory, and tactile senses (Aronoff, 1979).

The principal objectives of MYC are to build a solid foundation for understanding and enjoying music; nurture team skills through keyboard playing and rhythm ensemble; develop individual expressiveness through movement; reinforce music reading and theory with group activities and colorful, hands-on materials; integrate aural and written skills; and give a sense of ownership. The MYC accents the positive while refining the young child's listening, vocal, and fine- and gross-motor skills. Musical concepts are taught at the child's learning level and emphasis is placed on accuracy of basic skills to provide a solid foundation for further musical growth (Balodis, 1995). The MYC's primary goal is to encourage children to develop their enjoyment of music, and through work and play, spend much of their time involved in the activity of making music.

ORFF-SCHULWERK (CARL ORFF, 1895–1982, AND GUNILD KEETMAN, 1904–1990)

Orff-Schulwerk was started by German composer Carl Orff and his partner Gunild Keetman. Carl Orff's approach to music is based on the premise that feelings precede intellectual understanding (Raebeck & Wheeler, 1972). The child feels the sensations long before they are verbalized as ideas. When these inward sensations and feelings begin to form meanings for the child and are then verbalized, it is time to begin and write about them. The principal objectives of the Orff teaching method are that all students should find ways to express themselves through music, both as individuals and as members of a musical community (the ensemble). The musical experience itself is the most important objective (Choksy, 1999).

Orff believed that the easiest method of teaching music is to draw out the student's inherent affinities for rhythm and melody and allow these to develop in natural ways, leading the child by her intuition from primitive to more sophisticated expression through stages parallel to western music's evolution. He accomplishes this by means of a carefully planned program, beginning with speech patterns, rhythmic movement, and two-note tunes, and then moving logically into pentatonic melody. Adult pressure and mechanical drill are discouraged. Improvisation is encouraged. Major and minor melodies are introduced as the final stage of the program. Orff designed a special group of instruments, including glockenspiels, xylophones, metallophones, drums, and other percussion instruments, to fulfill the requirements of the Schulwerk courses. (*Schulwerk* is the German term for schooling or schoolwork.) The Orff Method's primary goal is to address every aspect of musical behavior: performing, creating, listening, and analyzing, through a variety of means (Frazee & Kreuter, 1987).

SUZUKI METHOD (SHINICHI SUZUKI, 1898–1998)

Shinichi Suzuki was born in Japan, the son of the owner of the largest violin factory in the world, and taught himself to play violin by listening to recordings of classical music. Suzuki discovered a way to develop musical ability in young children comparable to the way children develop their native tongue. He believed that children could learn to play a musical instrument in the same way that they first learn language. He also believed that a child's growth depends upon how she is raised and that education begins from birth, with emphasis on a strong child-parent learning relationship. Suzuki further believed that from birth, movement is the basis of all knowledge and intellectual performance (Wood, 2004).

The Suzuki Method challenges students to find ways to express themselves through music, both as individuals and as members of a musical community; encourages the parents of each child to provide music in the earliest stages of life; emphasizes that a child's capacities as a scholar will rest upon the earlier development of her whole being; suggests the child first learn to listen and hear each note accurately; recommends that the relationship of the parent to the child in a learning situation be warm; points to respect as the most important element in the relationship; and gives primary importance to the musical experience and the production of beautiful sound (Suzuki & Mills, 1973).

The Suzuki method builds upon the inherent nature of the child from birth and promotes providing an ideal home environment with parental support and participation at each lesson. Music to be learned should always be played for the child beforehand and followed by repetition by the child, which is followed with praise. One's future fate, or ability in later life, is determined by training in infancy and childhood (Suzuki & Mills, 1973). The Suzuki Method's primary goal is to work together to build a new human race.

What, Then, Is a Developmentally Appropriate Music Curriculum?

The following music-teaching approach, Mozart and the Young Mind (MYM), is specific to the very young child and has been tested through research. This developmentally appropriate music curriculum is based upon an understanding of the nature of learning and development of the young child. The MYM method provides instructional guidelines for early childhood educators in curriculum, child development, and assessment, and shows how to adapt curriculum and instruction to children's individual strengths, needs, and interests. Music concepts may be introduced to the preschool child in the following sequence.

1. Beat
    Beat vs. rhythm
2. Tempo
    Fast vs. slow
    Simple vs. duple
3. Dynamics
    Loud vs. soft
5. Rhythm
    Rhythm vs. beat
    ta-a-a-ah—whole note, *ta-ah*—half note, *tah*—quarter note, *ti-ti*—sixteenth notes
5. Pitch
    High vs. low
    Solfège
    Curwen hand signs
6. Harmony
    Monophonic singing
    Ostinato
7. Form
    Phrase
    Phrase form and mapping
8. Timbre
    Voice
    Body percussion
    Nonpitched percussion
    Pitched percussion
    Orchestral families
9. Expressive elements
    Staccato
    Legato

Specific lesson plans demonstrating these concepts can be found in chapter 9 and suggested materials are listed in chapter 10.

Mozart and the Young Mind

Mozart and the Young Mind (MYM) incorporates the leading approaches and philosophies that influence early childhood music and movement in education today and is sequenced to teach concepts of pitch, dynamics, duration, timbre, and form. It accents the positive while refining the young child's listening, vocal, and fine- and gross-motor skills.

The basic concepts toward which the teacher should be working during the early years of music education are listed above from simplest and easiest to the most complex and difficult. The sequence begins with song and follows through beat, tempo, rhythm, accent, dynamics, timbre, phrasing, and form to the introduction of musical styles from around the world.

Building depth in musical understanding takes time and requires thoughtful decisions on the part of the teacher regarding which musical styles to include in the music curriculum. Music styles to include are folk songs (lullabies and chants), traditional songs (ceremonial music and dance), western art music (instrumental and choral music from the baroque, classical, and Romantic periods), western twentieth-century musical theater and film music (Broadway, movie themes, etc.), and music from worldwide locales including Africa, Asia, the Middle East, and Australia.

Teachers combine keyboard, singing, rhythm, theory, and composition in each lesson to reinforce the teaching points of the lesson. Care is taken to provide gross-motor and fine-motor activities, and the lesson is designed with the child's attention span and abilities in mind. The length of the class period is not as important as the frequency—twenty- to thirty-minute sessions twice or thrice weekly with young children is more valuable than one forty-minute session once a week (Choksy, 1999).

This music program, developed by an early childhood music specialist, was designed to provide a child-centered musical environment to facilitate development in all curriculum areas, while enabling the child to learn fundamental music skills (Harris, 2005b). The program enhances a child's ability to learn concepts required in many disciplines while cultivating the child's own natural desire to learn, and this style of learning is directly compatible with the child learner–centered philosophy of education. Music, movement, rhythm, song, and drama, approached sequentially with step-by-step activities to benefit the whole child, are the basis of this program.

Creative movement develops individual expressiveness and coordination, while music skills are refined using group activities and hands-on music materials. Composing integrates aural and written skills and gives children a sense of ownership. Lastly, use of rhythm ensemble develops coordination, beat, and inner hearing, and nurtures self-confidence and communication skills. Movement builds a solid foundation of understanding and enjoyment of music while allowing the child to explore and develop her own strengths in a variety of musical areas (Gordon, 2003). The MYM program provides a child-centered musical environment to facilitate development in all curriculum areas, while enabling the child to learn fundamental music skills (Harris, 2005b).

Mozart and the Young Mind is specifically appropriate for the younger child. Gordon (2003) compares musical development to language development and states, ". . . because audiation is to musical performance what thought is to intelligent speaking, they will be deprived of learning the art of creating and improvising music. Their musical experiences in childhood and beyond most likely will be limited to simply following the thoughts, wishes, and directions of others" (p. 109).

Gordon (2003) states that children who have not acquired this music readiness will not succeed in formal instruction in school and will make little progress in music. He suggests that rather than starting every child in formal instruction in music, it is best to allow each child time to compensate for his deficiencies before beginning formal music instruction. This can be accomplished by one-on-one time between teacher and student. The child will enjoy listening to a teacher sing and chant just as he would enjoy listening to a teacher read. Unless children can sing in tune and move their bodies with good rhythm, they are not ready to begin taking instrumental lessons.

This developmentally appropriate music curriculum for young children is flexible enough to accommodate the diverse interests and learning styles of the child. The Mozart and the Young Mind method of independent learning places the educator as facilitator and co-learner. It builds upon the widely accepted standards set forth for each age level (National Association for the Education of Young Children, 2001a), maintains respect and recognition of the individual, and is taught in a flexible manner with opportunities for creativity and exploration.

The MYM method stands alone as a comprehensive early childhood music curriculum whose very core is based on valid research (Harris, 2004). Years of working with and following young children led to its evolution as a contemporary method of successfully introducing music to young children. Let's follow the research in both education and developmental psychology and adopt a music-enriched curriculum for our youngest minds.

these materials and present similarly to any introductory nomenclature card exercise. First, place the animal cards on the table, and when the animal sound is heard, the teacher points to the corresponding animal and says its name.

When introducing the hand signs for "Do, Re, Mi," it is important that the fist for *do* is placed at "belly button" or navel level, and that hand signs ascend from there as the sounds go higher. The children sit cross-legged while singing.

While the children remain sitting, introduce the two new songs "Freight Train" and "I Hear the Mill Wheel." Both songs begin with tapping a beat on the knees and introduce a different, quicker movement, such as crossing hand over hand to indicate quicker rhythmic patterns. For example, tap knees for the words "freight train," and cross hand over hand to tap opposite knees for the words "going," *pause*, "so fast," or tap knees for the words "I hear the mill wheel," and then hand over hand for the words "tic-a tic-a tac-a." The teacher may use her own movements; what is important is to demonstrate through movement that there is a rhythmic difference. Children should now be familiar with all of the hand actions for the song "Open, Shut Them," which is sung quietly.

NOVEMBER

Lesson Plan 3: Explore musical styles through dance and movement with scarves.

1. "Bombalalom"
2. "Here We Are Together"
3. "I'm in the Mood for Clapping"
4. "Wake Up Toes"
5. "Turn Around, Clap, Clap"
6. "A Ram Sam Sam"
7. Winter friends—chickadee, squirrel, coyote, cardinal
8. "Hot Cross Buns"
9. "Do You Know the Muffin Man?"
10. Beethoven—"Ode to Joy"—freeze
11. "Freight Train"
12. "Aiken Drum"
13. "Open, Shut Them"

To add further interest to the song "Here We Are Together" the children are invited to take a turn naming some of their friends sitting together. It is helpful to sing the children's names first, and then ask the child to name them in the same order. For the action song "I'm in the Mood for Clapping," ask the children for suggestions as to what they may be in the mood for—clapping, jumping, or tapping? During the song "Wake Up, Toes" the children are reminded that all of the body remains still, except for the body part waking up. The children then enjoy the last verse where the whole body moves to the words "wake up *me*." Winter friends are introduced with the nomenclature cards similar to the farm animals sounds. Any song where the children are expected to move and suddenly "freeze" (stop and hold the position for freeze), it is helpful to give the children prior warning by saying "get ready, we're going to freeze." "Do You Know the Muffin Man?" cultivates practice in correct vocal production, while "Hot Cross Buns" and "Freight Train" are now sung faster with each repeat, and tapping the beat while singing. "Aiken Drum" provides opportunities to emphasize story telling and vocabulary and is very much enjoyed when shakers are used during the chorus.

DECEMBER

Lesson Plan 4: Introduce world cultures and customs.

1. "Bombalalom"
2. "Here We Are Together"
3. "Mary's Wearing Her Red Dress"
    Intro to percussion bells and shakers

4. "Do, Re, Mi"
5. "Do, Re"
6. "Do, Re, Mi"
   Time signatures of 2/4 and 3/4
7. Handel's *Messiah*—dynamic expression
   Cultural celebrations around the world

While introducing the concepts and beliefs of different cultures, the teacher can use this opportunity to discuss the subject of rituals in various cultures. Perhaps the children can describe the ritual of their own religions?

The teacher can show the children how to chant by singing a sentence on one note and dropping the last note lower. Then invite the children to sing back what was just sung. One of the children can take the lead and sing a sentence, which is then echoed by the group. The children can now take turns being the leader and improvising on the chant as desired.

Over time, the children begin to internalize the accented beat of the music and experiment with movement, such as taking large steps to the music when slow, and shorter steps on the beat to quicker tempos. While moving to the accent of the music, ask the children, "Is this song a stepping song?" (those in 2/4 time), or "Is this song a skipping song?" (those in 6/8 time). Cards of varying meters such as 2/4, 3/4, 4/4, or 6/8 can be used for further practice of meter recognition.

JANUARY

Lesson Plan 5: Introduce percussion instruments (see lesson plans in chapter 9).

1. "Bombalalom"
2. "Here We Are Together"
3. "I'm in the Mood for Clapping"
4. "Wake Up, Toes"
5. "Clap, Clap, Clap"
6. "Do, Re, Mi"
7. "Do, Re"
8. "Do, Re, Mi"
9. Staccato and legato
10. "Clickety, Clickety, Clack"
11. "Scotland's Burning"
12. "Going to Kentucky"
13. "Sakura"—dance with scarves
14. "Ragtime"
15. Animal sounds—coyote, sheep, cardinal, horse, squirrel
16. "A Ram Sam Sam"
17. "I Hear the Mill Wheel"
18. "Freight Train"
19. "Toumba"—Israel
20. "Open, Shut Them"

Percussion playing comes in many forms and shapes, from body percussion to nonpitched instruments to pitched instruments. The teacher demonstrates the correct handling and playing of each instrument before introducing to the children (see lesson plans in chapter 9 for examples).

When using instruments, begin with nonpitched instruments all in resting position on the floor, then raise your hand to give the signal for each child to pick up the instrument immediately in front of him or her. The instruments are played for a short time to the beat of the music, for perhaps one verse of a song or four phrases in instrumental music. At this time, lower your hand, giving the children the signal to place their instruments in resting position. Now have each child pass the instrument to the child on his or her right, and the sequence is repeated, beginning with giving the signal to pick up the instruments again. Songs to introduce the playing of the instruments are "A Ram Sam Sam," "I Hear the Mill Wheel," "Freight

6. "Row, Row, Row Your Boat"—mapping
7. "Bombalalom"—mapping
8. "Open, Shut Them"

This month the children introduce themselves to each other through movement in the "Hello" song—"Hello, Hello, Hello, te-triple-te-trip-te-trip." Each child faces a partner and claps both hands on knees for the first half of the word "hel-lo" and raises hands and claps the partner's hands for the second half of "hel-lo." This is repeated twice. Looping opposite arms the children circle round each other for "te-triple-te-trip-te-trip." The movements are repeated for the next line in the song "Goodbye, goodbye, goodbye, te–triple-te-trip-te-trip." For the following few bars of music, each child moves around the room in search of a partner, stopping only when the music stops. Facing a new partner, the process is once again repeated. Some children need lots of practice in this game because it demands coordination, listening, time management, and so forth. The "Button and the Key" is a much-in-demand song by children of all ages and is a fun way to introduce the concept of "timbre." The children sit with eyes closed and listen to who answers the question asked "Who has the button?" and "Who has the key?" It is only through hearing that they must decide which friend the voice sounds like.

A musical phrase is similar to a sentence in language, usually four to eight bars in length followed by a natural breathing place. An extension of this exercise is mapping, where the children trace and draw the song form. Mapping the song on paper provides a visual representation of the phrasing of a song. Materials needed are large sheets of blank paper and large free-flowing markers for color. First, the children sing the song while sitting on the floor with paper and marker in front of them. Each child then uses his finger as a pointer, to practice drawing the song form. Repeat until the children are ready to draw their song form on the paper with a marker. Once the song form is completed, the song is sung again, while the children trace their drawings with their fingers. The children should reach the end of the drawing by the time they sing the end of the song. The song "Row, Row, Row Your Boat" is a visually simple song to map. For example, draw a zigzag pattern stopping on each word of "row, row, row your boat gently down the stream," and for "merrily, merrily, merrily, merrily" draw circular shapes, returning to the zigzag pattern for the last line of the song "life is but a dream." Mapping is multisensory because it connects listening, singing, seeing, moving, and touching all into one activity. It is the expression of the whole of the song as experienced.

MAY

Lesson Plan 9: Notation on the staff and dynamic cards.

1. "Hello"
2. "Down by the Bay"
3. "Scotland's Burning"
4. Gershwin—jazz/ragtime
5. "Row, Row, Row Your Boat"

The Mozart and the Young Mind teaching philosophy is based on establishing a concrete basis of knowledge before introducing abstract concepts. This belief is directly compatible with the now-popular sound-before-symbol teaching process in which the child experiences music aurally and kinesthetically before labeling and reading its symbolic representation. The child's education at which she is ready to move on to this stage of musical notation depends on the age and experience of the child. Many children at the early childhood level may be ready for formal notation, only to excel at it at the elementary level. As with all curriculum development, the teacher decides based on the child's knowledge of basic concepts and readiness to move on to more abstract concepts and introduces the appropriate materials at the child's various developmental stages.

JUNE

Lesson Plan 10: Exploration of creativity and improvisation.

1. Improvisation
2. Rounds

3. Playing bells from staff
4. Dance expression to music of Mozart, Beethoven, Prokofiev, Gershwin
5. Music of Africa, Asia, Europe, South America, Australia, Russia, North America, India
6. Solfège
7. Drum, echo, and improvisation

Singing rounds is an activity children enjoy and it should be introduced toward the end of the school year. The children should be very comfortable in singing the songs, on pitch, with accurate beat before attempting to sing in round. A round is a song that is sung by two (or three) groups simultaneously with one group starting usually two bars after the other. It is best for the children to begin singing first and for the teacher to join in quietly with the second part so that the children can hear the other part of the round but are not distracted by it and lose their singing place in the round. Once this is mastered, the children may divide into two groups singing the rounds, and later three groups with the assistance of the teacher. "Scotland's Burning" is a song very suitable to singing in rounds.

Improvisation and creativity in music and movement will flourish in a relaxed and accepting classroom where novel ideas and individual attempts are respected and encouraged. Improvisation can be explored through singing, timbre, rhythm, form, and melodic expression, while composing involves notating these creative musical ideas for later performances.

Including songs that are examples of sign language for children with hearing difficulties also educates the rest of the class in methods of communication. Children with hearing difficulties benefit from being included in music class. Through vibrations felt physically, the visual stimulation of watching an ensemble perform, and understanding the lyrics with signing, the music class becomes an exciting and enriching experience particularly for everyone including the hearing-impaired child.

Building Music Curriculum

Building depth in musical understanding takes time and requires thoughtful decisions on the part of the educator regarding which musical styles to include in the music curriculum. Music styles to include are folk songs (lullabies and chants), traditional songs (ceremonial music and dance), western art music (instrumental and choral music from the baroque, classical, and romantic periods), western twentieth-century musical theater and film music (Broadway, movie themes, etc.), and music from countries around the world, including Africa, Asia, the Middle East, and Australia.

Singing, keeping rhythm, playing the keyboard, and learning theory and composition are combined in each lesson to reinforce the teaching points of the lesson. Care is taken to provide gross-motor and fine-motor activities, and the lesson is designed with the child's attention span and abilities in mind. Composing integrates aural and written skills and gives children a sense of ownership. Lastly, participating in a rhythm ensemble develops coordination, beat, and inner hearing and nurtures self-confidence and communication skills. Rhythm ensemble playing builds a solid foundation of understanding and enjoyment of music while allowing the child to explore and develop his or her own strengths in a variety of musical areas (Gordon, 2003). Such rhythm playing provides a child-centered musical environment to facilitate development in all curriculum areas, while enabling the child to learn fundamental music skills (Harris, 2005b).

Music educators who work with young children and infants have found that the best way to meet the musical developmental needs of the young child is to create an environment and opportunity for the child to express himself through movement, whether creative or structured. When the child enters an early childhood classroom, the use of music as a spontaneous expression continues from that experienced at home, and the teacher gradually introduces the elements of music in a more structured way. This developmentally appropriate music curriculum for young children is flexible enough to accommodate the diverse interests and learning styles. Mozart and the Young Mind places the educator as facilitator and colearner. It builds upon the widely accepted standards set forth for each age level (National Association for the Education of Young Children, 2001b), maintains respect and recognition of the individual, and is taught in a flexible manner with opportunities for creativity and exploration.

Dynamics: Loud-Soft

Ample practice at keeping a steady beat is recommended before progressing to this exercise.

♪♪♪

Material: Singing voice and/or recorded music
Purpose/Aim: Dynamic discrimination
                    Dynamic production

♪♪♪

PRESENTATION

In initial performances of the song, the teacher should vary the dynamics quite distinctly changing from very loud (*fortissimo*) to very soft (*pianissimo*) to assist the children in gauging the differences they hear in the dynamics as accurately as possible. The children can demonstrate the differences with movement—perhaps standing big like an elephant when hearing loud music, and becoming small like a mouse when hearing music played softly.

♪♪♪

VARIATIONS

Loud and soft can also be demonstrated by singing a song very softly to the children, without comment, as something for them to listen to, such as "Hush Little Baby." After they have heard the song a number of times, invite the children to sing it. Ask them to describe how the song makes them feel: "sleepy," "quiet," and "soft"? This "soft" song should now be compared with a song of very different character—one the children have sung in a much louder voice, such as "Going to Kentucky."

Musical Vocabulary

The words "medium," "loud," "louder," and "medium," "soft," "softer" assist in developing a musical vocabulary.

Percussion instruments

Have children tap softly when hearing music played at *p* and loudly to music played at *f*. Most children tend to speed up when playing loudly and slow down when playing softly.

Notation

Dynamic notation and the use of cards take children from the concrete to the abstract. The dynamic differences are no longer demonstrated by movement, which is replaced by a visual representation of the terminology used to describe dynamic levels.

Timbre (TAM-B∃R)

The term "timbre" refers to *the tone color* of an instrument or voice.

♪♪♪

Material: The child
Purpose/Aim: Timbre discrimination, production, and composition

♪♪♪

PRESENTATION

The timbre of the voice refers to the quality of the sound produced. The simplest example of timbre is the difference between the sounds produced by the reed instruments (e.g., clarinet compared to that of the oboe) or the difference between the sound of a man's voice and that of a young child.

A good exercise for teaching timbre discrimination is to have children sit in a circle with eyes closed while listening to the sound of each other's voice as each child takes a turn saying his or her name. To add further to the discrimination of timbre, have a child attempt to disguise his voice by saying his name differently. In each exercise, the sounds are similar with the tone or timbre giving the sound its unique distinguishable quality.

♪♪♪

VARIATIONS

Games

Playing the game "Button and the Key" (see appendix B) encourages careful listening skills as the children answer with their name; over time resort to disguising their sounds by either whispering, shouting, talking, or singing.

Body percussion

The most accessible and easily manipulated means of producing sound is the child's own body. Using the body as an instrument to make different sounds—such as snapping, clapping, or stamping—to highlight text is always enjoyed.

Instruments

Another means of producing different sounds is through the use of various percussion instruments. They can be used to distinguish timbre—whether it is metal, wood, or skin. Eventually the children should be able to name the instrument they hear with eyes closed.

Music sound shakers

Sound shakers are easily made to produce different degrees of sound, such as filling small plastic shakers with rice, pasta, pebbles, stones, etc. Creating shakers in sets of two offers an exercise in matching, while introducing each set as different sounds offers a further exercise in differentiation.

Live performances

Live musical performances are usually the most powerful medium through which children can experience the timbre of orchestral instruments. There are many opportunities for the young child to experience live performances, for example, family performances at home, college music students who are willing to come to school and demonstrate orchestral instruments, or parents with knowledge of their cultural music genre can come into the classroom to offer the children a personal connection with music from other cultures.

─ɯ─ Percussion Instruments ─ɯ─
Wooden Nonpitched Instruments

Rhythm Sticks

♪♪♪

Material: Rhythm sticks
Purpose/Aim: Introduction to rhythm sticks instrument
Aural recognition of instrument
Visual recognition and naming of instrument
Demonstration of use of instrument

♪♪♪

PRESENTATION

Select the rhythm sticks from among the percussion instruments. Pick them up and rest both of them in the palm of one hand with the other hand holding the extended sticks securely. Carry them to a rug and carefully place them down without making any noise. Sit down, place hands in lap, look at the rhythm sticks lying on the rug, and say "resting position." Gently pick up one stick with the left hand and the remaining stick with the right hand, and say "rhythm sticks." While the left hand firmly holds the rhythm stick in a horizontal position from the body, strike it gently in the middle with the other rhythm stick held in the right hand. The sound dies immediately. Signal to the children that there is silence. Return the rhythm sticks, left hand stick first, followed by remaining right hand stick, to their place on the rug and invite the children to take turns. When finished, one child returns the rhythm sticks to their place on the shelf.

♪♪♪

VARIATIONS

All wooden nonpitched instruments

Continue to present more wooden nonpitched instruments until the children are familiar with the name, sound, and correct use of each instrument.

Categorizing

The percussion instruments can also be categorized by materials used—metal, wood, or skin.

Maracas, Wooden

♩♩♪

Material: Maraca
Purpose/Aim: Introduction to a Latin American instrument
                Aural recognition of instrument
                Visual recognition and naming of instrument
                Demonstration of use of instrument

♩♩♪

PRESENTATION

Select a maraca from among the percussion instruments. Pick it up and carry it with the head cradled in the palm of one hand and the fingers of the other hand holding the handle. Carry it to a rug and carefully place it down without making any noise. Sit down, place hands in lap, look at the maraca lying on the rug, and say "resting position." Gently pick it up, say "maraca," and then shake it above your head. Keep listening until the sound can no longer be heard and repeat the process twice more. Return the maraca to its place on the rug and invite the children to take turns. When finished, one child returns the maraca to its place on the shelf.

VARIATIONS

The maraca can also be played by gently tapping it against the palm of the hand.

All wooden nonpitched instruments

Continue to present more wooden nonpitched instruments until the children are familiar with the name, sound, and correct use of each instrument.

Categorizing

Using cards, the percussion instruments and cards can be categorized by materials used—metal, wood, or skin.

Auditory discrimination

The percussion instruments can be categorized by the quality of the sound produced. For all exercises, once demonstrated, invite the children to take turns.

Wood Block

Material: A wood block
Purpose/Aim: Introduction to wood block instrument
                 Aural recognition of instrument
                 Visual recognition and naming of instrument
                 Demonstration of use of instrument

PRESENTATION

Select a wood block from among the percussion instruments. Pick it up and carry it in the palm of one hand and the fingers of the other hand placed gently on top to hold securely. Carry it to a rug and carefully place it down without making any noise. Return and pick out a wooden-tipped mallet and carry it carefully with the head cradled in the palm of one hand and the fingers of the other hand holding the handle. Sit down, place hands in lap, look at the wood block lying on the rug, and say "resting position." Gently pick it up with left hand and say "wood block." Now pick up the mallet with the right hand and say "mallet." Balance the wood block in the palm of the hand and strike with the mallet. It produces a loud knocking sound. Repeat the process twice more. Return the wood block and mallet to the rug and invite the children to take turns. When finished, one child returns the wood block to its place on the shelf, and then returns the mallet to its place on the shelf.

VARIATIONS

All wooden nonpitched instruments

Continue to present more wooden nonpitched instruments until the child is familiar with the name, sound, and correct use of each instrument.

All skin nonpitched instruments

Continue to present more skin nonpitched instruments until the child is familiar with the name, sound, and correct use of each instrument.

All metal nonpitched instruments

Continue to present more metal nonpitched instruments until the child is familiar with the name, sound, and correct use of each instrument.

Categorizing

The percussion instruments can also be categorized by materials used—metal, wood, or skin.

Auditory discrimination

The percussion instruments can be categorized by the quality of the sound produced.

Hand Drum

♪♪♪

Material: Hand drum
Purpose/Aim: Introduction to hand drum instrument
                 Aural recognition of instrument
                 Visual recognition and naming of instrument
                 Demonstration of use of instrument

♪♪♪

PRESENTATION

Select a hand drum from among the percussion instruments. Pick it up and carry it in the palm of one hand and the fingers of the other hand placed gently on top to hold securely. Carry it to a rug and carefully place it down without making any noise. Sit down, place hands in lap, look at the hand drum lying on the rug, and say "resting position." Sit cross-legged and with both hands pick up the hand drum and place it on the floor. Hold the drum by the rim with left hand and gently tap the skin side with the fingertips, or ball of hand. Repeat the process twice more. Return the hand drum to its place on the rug and invite the children to take turns. When finished, one child returns the hand drum to its place on the shelf.

♪♪♪

VARIATIONS

Conga Drum

Sit cross-legged and pick up the conga drum with both hands and place it on the floor between your legs. Hit the skin of the drum with the whole hand, fingertips, or heel of hand, or knuckles. The produced sound varies depending on how and where the player hits the skin. Repeat the process twice more.

Bongo Drums

Introduce the Latin American bongo drums in the same manner as the conga drums.

All skin nonpitched instruments

Continue to present more skin nonpitched instruments until the child is familiar with the name, sound, and correct use of each instrument.

Categorizing

The percussion instruments can also be categorized by materials used—metal, wood, or skin.

Auditory discrimination

The percussion instruments can be categorized by the quality of the sound produced.

Metal Pitched Instruments

Jingle Bells

♪♪♪

Material: Jingle bells
Purpose/Aim: Introduction to bell instrument
                   Aural recognition of instrument
                   Visual recognition and naming of instrument
                   Demonstration of use of instrument

♪♪♪

PRESENTATION

Select a jingle bell from among the percussion instruments. Pick it up and carry it with the head cradled in the palm of one hand and the fingers of the other hand holding the handle. Carry it to a rug and carefully place it down without making any noise. Sit down, place hands in lap, look at the jingle bell lying on the rug, and say "resting position." Gently pick it up, say "jingle bell," and then shake it gently in the air. Keep listening until the sound can no longer be heard and repeat the process twice more. Return the jingle bell to its place on the rug and invite the children to take turns. When finished, one child returns the jingle bell to its place on the shelf.

♪♪♪

VARIATIONS

Tambourine

Gently pick it up by grasping the wooden side with thumb and four fingers of dominant hand, say "tambourine," and then firmly tap the instrument against the side of the body. Keep listening until the sound can no longer be heard and repeat the process twice more. Return the tambourine, flat side down, to its place on the rug and invite the children to take turns. You may need to assist the children in using the correct grasp to pick up the tambourine. When finished, one child returns the tambourine to its place on the shelf.

Triangle

Using the left hand gently lift the triangle and suspend the instrument from the attached string. Lift the metal striker with the right hand and strike the edge of the triangle. Keep listening until the sound can no longer be heard and repeat the process twice more. Return the triangle to the rug and place the metal mallet to its right side and invite the children to take turns. When finished, one child replaces the triangle and metal striker to the case and returns it to its place on the shelf.

Xylophone

The xylophone is an excellent instrument to demonstrate pitch presentations.

♪ Pitched Instruments ♪

The piano or keyboard are members of the percussion family of instruments and are thus included in this section. Although a three-year-old enjoys the exploration of the keyboard and its basic principles, formal instruction is usually recommended for the slightly older child.

Keyboard

Set up a keyboard on a table that is placed against a wall in such a manner that the keyboard can only be viewed from the front. If an electrical outlet is used, ensure it is tucked away and safe from the inquisitive fingers of the child. The chair that is placed in front of the keyboard is at a height that enables the child to sit down, extend her hands at right angle from her body, and rest the hands on the keys.

♪♪♪

Material: Keyboard
Purpose/Aim: Introduction to keyboard
                     Demonstration of use of instrument

♪♪♪

PRESENTATION

Sit down at keyboard with back straight and arms extended to rest curved fingers on keys. Show the children how to turn on the keyboard. Explain that there are many uses for keys, such as opening locks and starting cars. The keyboard keys make a sound when pushed down. Hold right hand in curved position and gently press any key with the middle finger. Now it is the child's turn. Ensure hand position is correct and show the children how to press every key on the keyboard. Start with the lowest note to the left of the keyboard, press gently with third finger and listen. Lift hand and move to the next note to the right and once again press with third finger. Continue to the last note and invite the children to take turns. When finished, turn off the keyboard and push in chair.

♪♪♪

VARIATIONS

Finger strength

Continue to present all notes using different fingers and both hands.

Recognizing left from right

Establish right and left hand and the ability to differentiate between the two hands: The right hand usually plays the higher notes to the right of the keyboard, while the left hand plays the lower notes to the left.

Keyboard—White and Black Keys

Material: Keyboard
Purpose/Aim: Recognition of white keys and black keys
                 Introduction to "two" or "three" black keys

PRESENTATION

Demonstrate to the children the patterns of black keys on the keyboard by pointing to all the groups of three black notes and exaggerate skipping over each group of two black notes. Invite the children to point to each set of three black notes. Once mastered, invite the children to point to each set of two black notes.

Holding either hand in a curved position press a group of three black notes with three fingers and listen to the sound. Skip the group of two black notes to the right and press the next group of three. Continue this pattern up and down (left to right and back again) the keyboard and invite the children to do likewise.

VARIATIONS

Group recognition

Once recognition of groups is established randomly ask the children to play a group of three or two black notes.

Finger playing

When playing the piano each finger is designated a specific number. Introduce the right hand with thumb being finger no. 1 over to the pinky finger, which is no. 5. Introduce the left hand in a similar fashion with thumb being finger no. 1 through to pinky finger being no. 5. Once recognition of fingering is established ask the children to play a note on the keyboard using a specific finger of either hand. Ensure that the correct hand position is being used—elbow to knuckles are in a straight horizontal position with fingers relaxed and curved.

Improvisation

Encourage the children to create their own sounds by exploring the notes on the keyboard. They may be willing to share their composition with friends.

Playing by ear

Perhaps the children would like to play a familiar easy melody. Children often become entranced with this task especially when it is their sensitive period for learning.

Bell Material

Bell Material—Set Up

The bell is an excellent percussion instrument to demonstrate some of the following music concepts.

Using two different sets of bells, set up on a table or shelf which is placed against a wall in such a manner that the bells can only be viewed from the front. Choose sets of bells in two different colors and place one set in front of the other. I have chosen a white set of bells as the control set (they are never moved from the original correct set-up position and are placed at the back) and a blue set of bells placed in front that can be moved as necessary. Place a mallet with a firm rubber head and a damper to the right side of the bells.

Bell presentations begin with the auditory reinforcement of the musical scale played from left to right, lowest to highest. Play up the blue bells (left to right) and down the white bells (right to left). The scale sound produced should match the scale produced on a keyboard beginning on the note C and playing up to the right and back down to C.

If bells are marked underneath with pitch letters, the order is C–D–E–F–G–A–B–C from left to right.

Bell Material Terminology

- Bell–Bells are a dual chromatic set including single-color controls. The pitch runs from middle C to high C, including the sharps.
- Mallet—the object used to strike the bell (a firm rubber mallet head produces a pure sound)
- Damper—the object used to stop the tone of the bell

The children are to stand while playing the bells in order to keep the arm parallel to the floor while striking the bells. The educator may need to kneel when first presenting the bell material to the children.

Speaking is kept to a minimum in all presentations in order to allow the children to focus completely without distractions. It is of great importance during any bell presentation that the human voice does not intrude and divert the children's focus from the pure tone of the bells.

When introducing any musical concept, keep in mind the need to demonstrate lowest to highest, in preparation for music theory.

Bell Material—Carry a Bell

♪♪♪

Material: Music bells
Purpose/Aim: Introduction to bell material
                 Carrying a bell

♪♪♪

PRESENTATION

From the bell table select a blue bell by picking it up at the stem with the thumb, second, and third fingers of one hand, and immediately placing the palm of the other hand underneath the base of the bell. Turn around and walk toward the children, carefully carrying the bell. Gently place the bell on a table ensuring that no sound is made in the process. Gesture to the children that you are listening for sound and then shake your head to indicate there is no sound to be heard.

Return to the bell cabinet and select the mallet by picking it up with the thumb, second and third fingers of one hand, and immediately placing the palm of the other hand underneath the head of the mallet. Walk to the single bell and gently place the mallet on the table beside the bell. Say the word "mallet."

Return to the bell cabinet and select the damper and hold it horizontally with the other hand. Strike the bell with the mallet, acknowledge the beautiful sound, and with the other hand stop the sound by lifting up the damper and pressing the felt end of the damper to the lower edge of the rim of the bell. Indicate to the children that you are listening for a sound and there is only silence. Repeat this process and invite the children to take turns. Ensure each child is holding the damper with the felt side facing upward.

Bell Material—Matching Pitch

♪♪♪

Material: Music bells
Purpose/Aim: Matching bell pitches
                 Development of pitch memory
                 Development of inner hearing

♪♪♪

PRESENTATION

Bell presentations begin with the auditory reinforcement of the musical scale played from left to right, lowest to highest. Play up the blue bells (left to right) and down the white bells (right to left). The scale sound produced should match the scale produced on a keyboard beginning on the note C and playing up to the right and back down to C. Using the first, fourth, and seventh blue bells, take the first bell and place it in front toward the right end of the bell setup. Place the fourth bell to the left of the bell just moved. Now place the seventh bell to the left of the second bell just moved (Fig. 9.1).

Figure 9.1.   White Montessori bells with first, fourth, and seventh blue bells in front at right end.

Now proceed to present in a manner similar to any matching exercise. Using the white bells as the control, strike the lowest white bell first and then from the three bells in the front strike the bell to the left. Listen carefully and shake head to indicate that these sounds do not match. Once again, strike the white control bell, listen, strike another blue bell, listen, and shake head to indicate the two sounds do not match. Repeat this process with the last blue bell, and nod head to indicate yes when the sounds match. Take the matching blue bell with two hands and place carefully in front of the white space to the far left of the bell setup (Fig. 9.2). Repeat this process for the remaining fourth and seventh blue bells.

Figure 9.2.   Blue bell placed in front of white space to far left of bell setup.

Now that the three blue bells are placed in front of their matching white bells, check each match by striking the white bell first and then the corresponding blue bell. Once the pitches match, place the blue bell onto its white space (Fig. 9.3). Once all bells have been returned to the original place, check once more by playing up the blue bells and down the white.

♪ ♪ ♪

VARIATION

Increase the number of bells used.

Figure 9.3.   Blue bell placed onto its white space.

Bell Material—Ascending and Descending

♪♪♪

Material:	Music bells
Purpose/Aim:	Introduction to ascending scale
	Introduction to descending scale
	Development of listening skills
	Preparation for high and low sounds

♪♪♪

PRESENTATION

After checking the bells, pause and slowly play from left to right the ascending scale on the blue bells. After each note, say "higher," "higher," etc. After playing the last bell return and play the scale once more saying when finished, "the sounds are getting higher while going up the scale." Play the descending scale from right to left and say, "the sounds are getting lower while going down the scale."

♪♪♪

VARIATIONS

High and Low

The largest possible contrast in pitch is between the first bell—the lowest—and the seventh bell. The eighth bell is one octave higher (or first overtone) than the first bell and the pitch difference is not as easily heard. After checking the bells, move the two chosen bells out in front of their white spaces. Strike the low tone (furthest to the left) with the mallet, listen carefully, and then stop the tone with the damper. On the same pitch sing, "this is a low bell." Now introduce the high bell and sing on the same pitch "this is a high bell." Return the bells to their original position and place mallet and damper in their place to the side of the bell setup.

Grading

Play bells ascending and descending. Take the blue bells and move in front of bell setup in mixed formation. Play the first bell C of the white control bells and find its match in the blue bells. Place the matching C bell on its space. Now find the D bell using the same procedure. You are now ready to grade the remaining bells. Repeat this process until all bells are graded and returned to their place; verify the scale by playing up the scale and back down again. Play the blue bells to hear if they have been successfully graded.

Music and movement

Many games, dances, and songs lend themselves to demonstrating the ascending and descending patterns with body movements. For example, begin in a crouched down position and gradually lift the body until standing really tall and trying to touch the sky. Reverse the action and slowly descend down into a crouched position.

Bell Material—Major Scale

♪♪♪

Material: Music bells
Purpose/Aim: Visual recognition of the scale

♪♪♪

PRESENTATION

(1) Major scale recognition: Play the bells and ask the children to sing what they just heard using "la." Strike the first bell and sing on the same pitch, "do." Strike the second bell and sing on the same pitch "re." Strike the thirrd bell and sing on the same pitch "me." Sing one of the three pitches and ask the children which note did you sing, *do, re,* or *mi*? Continue until solfège for the complete scale is introduced. (2) Hand signs: Hand signs are introduced in a similar presentation as solfège (find a picture of the Curwen-Kodály hand signs at www.classicsforkids.com/teachers/training/handsigns.asp). The fist for low *do* is placed at the belly button position, and all other hand signs move upward from there. High *do* (the highest note) is shown using the hand sign above head. Continue demonstrating the specific hand sign for each pitch of the scale.

♪♪♪

VARIATIONS

Descending scale

Present the above in descending order beginning with the highest note and grade pitch, moving down in descending order.

Scale memorization

Mix the bells on a table and place in a straight line. Take two bells and compare both. Take the lower sounding of the two bells and place to the left. Take another bell compare both. Take the lower sounding of the two bells and place to the left. Continue to the end of the line, and the last bell on the right should be the highest of all. Play all bells from left to right to verify the scale.

Movement games

Children line up according to the degree of the scale they represent. This is accomplished by either holding a bell and lining up according to the bell pitch placement in the scale, or holding specific pitch cards, or hand sign cards and lining up according to the specific scale placement of each card.

Bell Material—Chromatic Scale Pattern

♪♪♪

Material: Music bells
Purpose/Aim: Introduction to chromatic scale

♪♪♪

PRESENTATION

(1) Keyboard: Show the child how to play the chromatic scale on the keyboard by starting on the note C and playing all black and white notes through to the next C, explaining that each note is followed by the next closest sounding note. (2) Whole tones: The introduction of whole tones, semitones, and tetra chords, and so on, is introduced in the next level of Mozart and the Young Mind—for the elementary student. (2) Movement: One group of children represents the white keys on the keyboard, and another group of children represent the black keys on the keyboard. Line up three children from left to right (the white keys) and place footstools or overturned boxes in between each of the three children. Ask two children from the black key group to come forward and stand on the footstools. Continuing from left to right add five more children from the white key group and invite three children from the black key group to come forward. Bring attention to the placement of the three new footstools and place them between children on white keys 4 and 5, 5 and 6, and 6 and 7. Do not place a stepstool between white-key children 3 and 4, and white-key children 7 and 8. Invite the three children from the black-key group to stand on the footstools. Show the children that there is *no* footstool or child between numbers 3 and 4 and 7 and 8, just as it is on the keyboard. The black keys are arranged in groups of three and two leaving some of the white keys without any black keys in between. This is where the half tones, or semitones, lie; they are discussed in further depth in Mozart and the Young Mind—for the elementary student.

─᷍─ Music Notation Material ─᷍─

The music notation materials bring the child from the concrete to the abstract study of music and are the next step in the curriculum. This material is only introduced to the child after a solid foundation in the previous exercises is reached. The following materials can be produced by the classroom teacher or purchased from any music material supply company.

The Staff and Clefs

♩♩♪

Materials: Staff boards, or five lines drawn
            Treble clef
            Bass clef
            5 discs numbered 1–5
            4 discs numbered 1–4
Purpose/Aim: Representation of the sounds heard on staff.

♩♩♪

PRESENTATION

Introduce the staff as five lines and four spaces. Trace from left to right the bottom line, say "one" and place a no. 1 disc on the line. Trace the second line and place disc no. 2. Continue to the top line and use the same procedure to introduce the four spaces.

Place the treble clef on the table beside the green board and trace its shape with index finger. Invite the child to trace the shape and say "treble clef." Explain that this clef has a very specific place on the green board and place it so that the curved part of the bottom rests on the first line of the staff and the end of the curve rests on the second line of the staff.

Place bass clef (also known as the F Clef) on the table beside the green board and trace its shape. Invite the child to trace the shape and say "bass clef." Explain that this clef has a very specific place on the green board and place it so that the curved part of the top rests on the top fifth line of the staff and the end of the curve rests on the fourth line of the staff.

♩♩♪

VARIATIONS

Drawing

Create workbooks for the children to practice tracing and drawing treble and bass clefs.

Movement

Create the staff on the floor or outside on the grass. Provide children with all the discs 1 through 5 and announce that when you call a line or space the child holding that specific numbered disc moves to the line or space it represents on the staff.

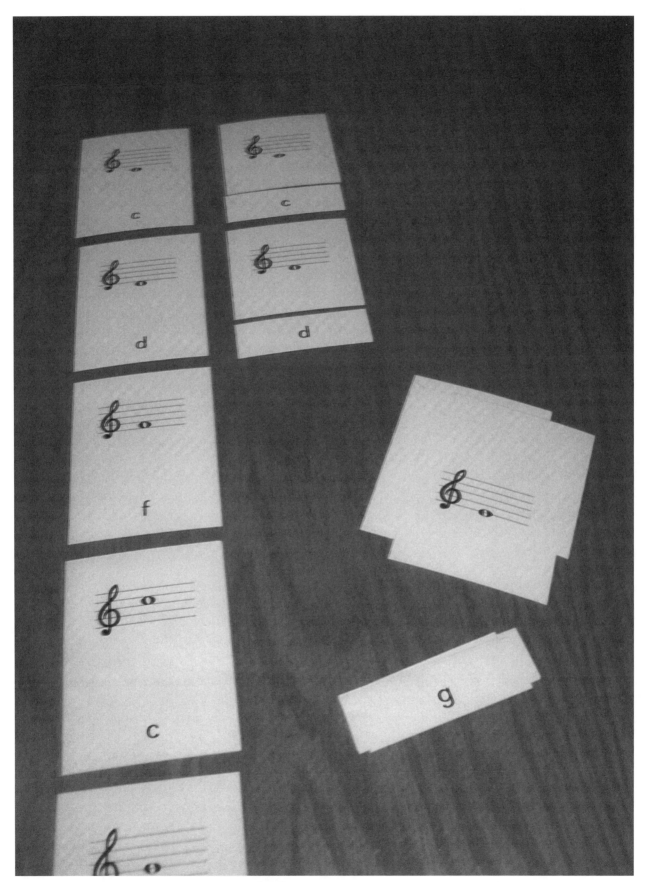

Figure 9.6. Scale flashcards arranged vertically

Note Values

♪♪♪

Material: Music note cards
Purpose/Aim: Introduction to note values
                 Music vocabulary

♪♪♪

PRESENTATION

(1) From the music note cards, place the card representing the quarter note (solid black note with stem) on the table. Clap once and indicate one beat. Place the half note card (black note with white center with stem) on the table. Clap once and leaving hands together in a small motion move them forward away from body and back. Indicate two beats. Place the whole note card (black note with white center) on the table. Clap once and leaving hands together in a small motion move them forward away from the body, pulse three times, and return. Indicate four beats.

• Quarter note = 1 beat
• Half note = 2 beats
• Whole note = 4 beats

The clap counts as one of the beats followed by a pulse for the remaining beats.

(2) Rest Values: Present as above for the note values. Instead of clapping, hands are opened wide apart and pulsed for the required number of beats.

♪♪♪

VARIATIONS

Repeating the music note value presentation above, introduce the name of the notes. For the rest values say "quarter note rest" for the one-beat rest, a "half note rest" for the two-beat rest, and a "whole note rest" for the four-beat rest.

Dynamics

Bring dynamic cards to the table and place the card for loud (*f*) on the table and say "forte" in a loud voice. Next take the card marked (*mf*) place on table and say "mezzoforte" in a moderately loud speaking voice. Take the card marked *p*, place on table, and say "piano" in a whispering voice. Continue to reinforce the musical dynamic vocabulary.

Movement

Children enjoy creatively moving to express note values and rests. Encourage the children to use their imaginations when working together musically.

⎯ᚾ⎯ Creativity and Improvisation ⎯ᚾ⎯

Creative Movement

♪♪♪

Material: High-quality recordings or live musicians
Purpose/Aim: Introduce improvisation in music and movement

♪♪♪

PRESENTATION

Creative movement is an enjoyable way for children to explore movement through music. It provides all children with a positive environment for the exploration of creative experiences, regardless of age, gender, race, or development stage. When a child responds to the sounds with motion, through swaying, clapping, or rocking from side to side, he is developing and exploring his innate creativity. Within this interactive environment and the use of props such as scarves, balloons, and feathers, the child learns to share space with his friends and subsequently develops higher levels of awareness of himself and others.

Sitting for extended periods of time may be difficult for some children and providing the child with opportunities for music and movement relieves stress and tension and a need to release energy.

♪♪♪

Finally, I believe that the cultivation of mutual respect for oneself and others is of utmost importance to creating a peaceful civilization. Experiences in music and movement can help children learn to recognize, appreciate, and respect differences in the people they meet. They become more aware of themselves, more sensitive to others, and actively conscious of the world they share.

Above all, teachers' enjoyment of music should be abundantly clear. Music brings people together through shared experiences; it reminds us of special times and comforts us when we are sad, lonely, or remorseful. Melodies will bring to mind friends, family, and special memories. Music brings us pleasure and joy because it helps define who we are as people.

It is my hope that these suggestions will aid the early childhood educator in using creative movement to enhance the rhythm of the classroom.

> The child is his own instrument. He can choreograph the ballet, direct the orchestra, be the dancer and the audience if we free him to play with the song, to have the song in him and lead him to explore it. Through movement and exploration of the song with his peers, the possibilities for growth are unlimited. He needs no other equipment than himself—not a piano nor a CD nor a computer. Each child can respond with his whole being—his brain, his body, his emotions, and he can interiorize all the sounds of the music and the language. He can sing all the wonderful, simple songs any time, anywhere. Nothing is needed to get him started but the child himself, a group of his peers, and you to lead him and show him the way.
>
> —Mary Helen Richards (Education Through Music)

- How to introduce the instruments of the orchestra
- How to introduce musical bells
- How to teach improvisation and composing
- How to introduce music symbols and notation

This developmentally appropriate music curriculum is flexible enough to accommodate the diverse interests and multicultural learning styles of the young child, and this method of independent learning places the educator as facilitator and co-learner with the freedom to expand and include learning for all children. It builds upon the widely accepted standards set forth for educating the young child (NAEYC, 2004), maintains respect and recognition of the individual, and is taught in a friendly, flexible manner with opportunities for multicultural creativity and exploration (Harris, 2005).

Following the step-by-step curriculum guide in chapters 8 and 9, teachers can run the beginning early childhood music and movement classes smoothly. The accompanying CD provides the basic melody, pitch, and rhythm for all the songs in the text and provides the new music educator with the tools to teach with confidence. For the more experienced educator, this guide can be expanded based on the children's music and movement responses. Over time, it is the flexibility of this curriculum that sets it aside from instruction that is more traditional. Inexperienced educators can follow closely the detailed lesson plans with ease; and use them to gain confidence in their abilities to spontaneously respond and improvise depending on the children's activities. It is this musical confidence and response that provide the springboard for exhilarating future music experiences between educator and child.

Tricks of the Trade

Now that the environment for teaching music is prepared, and the educator is confidently following the step-by-step Mozart and the Young Mind curriculum detailed in chapters 8 and 9, I want to share some practical and commonsense suggestions acquired from many years of experience teaching the young child.

In a typical early childhood classroom, parents leave the child with the educator. The child settles into the routine, becomes comfortable with the surrounding environment and friends, and adapts easily to the routine. Some children find transition times difficult; moving from one room to another, or going outside or to the music room may become stressful to them. Seeing a familiar face (the classroom teacher or assistant) throughout the process can ease the transition, especially if a music specialist is working with the children and lessons take place in the music room.

A quality audio system that can be heard clearly around the room should be placed out of the reach of the children, while an individual listening area off to the side can accommodate the older children working on independent projects. The use of puppets to dramatize a musical story or text of a song are helpful tools in engaging the young child and act as visual props. Some children are not comfortable holding hands in group settings, and using a stretchable ribbon or Hula-hoop for everyone to grasp may alleviate unnecessary anxiety for the shyer child. Scarves and streamers used for demonstrating phrasing and form are excellent props to use with the child who is not comfortable with movement activities.

Class control is rarely a problem if the educator is prepared, knows the children, anticipates behavior, is flexible, and keeps the lesson FUN! From the moment the educator decides it is now time for music, a positive attitude prevails. Announce to the children with a smile and excitable voice, "Children, we are now going to do something really special. [*pause*] It is time for music. Let's tidy up and come together." The teacher now sits on the floor quietly singing, beckoning to the children to join her, while the assistant helps those children in need. Usually the children are curious as to what the teacher is doing and attracted to the sound of the beautiful soft singing, and without any reminders, they will come unescorted and sit down with her. Eventually any stragglers, seeing their friends sitting, will join the group out of curiosity—the educator has simply sat and sung all the while. Facial expressions are also important, making eye contact with the children while continuously smiling and patting the floor beside you gives direction as to the expected behavior to come and sit down.

Choosing a leader, someone who demonstrates the movement actions to particular songs, assists in including the child who is not listening or acting inappropriately during class. The insecure and introverted child responds well to sitting close to a friend, while the busy, extroverted child may need to sit opposite that special friend.

Flexibility in the teachers' direction can also offset behavioral issues. No matter what the lesson plan is for the day, if for whatever reason the children are being distracted, simply do something different. If all are sitting, stand and say, "Let's now stand and sing 'Going to Kentucky.' This is such a fun song. Who is going to be the leader for this song?" If a movement song is getting a little out of hand, turn off the music, sit down, and whisper, "This is my favorite song. Come join me in singing 'Open, Shut Them,'" and immediately begin singing in a soft voice. Once again, the child is mesmerized by the pure sound of the human voice, and when singing quietly, it brings down the volume of noise in the room as the children stop to listen. Without any shouting or clapping on the part of the educator, the students have now returned to a sitting position and are listening intently to the song. The teacher has regained the attention of the group and can immediately move on to the next step in the lesson.

Keeping the children engaged and participating in a fun manner is the best method to offset silly behavior for young children who developmentally need to explore their surrounding environment. They are wonderful students to work with since their enthusiasm for learning and newness is endless, and it is the duty of the educator to make all these first experiences positive. To do so, continuing the lessons in a fun manner keeps the child engaged, and the research clearly shows that children who are engaged perform at higher levels (Harris, 2006; Upitis et al., 2001). For some children, their only exposure to music may lie in the hands of the educator, and experiences at such a young age have a profound effect on future development. Children who are happy and having fun enjoy learning, and discipline problems remain at a minimum.

Percussion instruments are so interesting to children that quite often they want to use them all or show preference for the instrument the child sitting next to them is using. As discussed in chapter 9, correct use of each instrument is demonstrated and practiced, and when ready, the children take turns using all the instruments. Place an instrument on the floor in front of each of the children, reminding them to leave the instruments in resting position. If a child picks up the instrument, simply turn and say, "the instruments remain in resting position until all of us are ready to use them. Do you need my help or can you return it to resting position yourself?" To give the children as many opportunities as possible to explore the instruments, pause the music between each verse of a song, ask the children to pass their instrument to the child beside them. (This takes a little time in the beginning, and the educator will need to show the child how to pass the instrument to the child on the *right*.) Once the children are used to passing the instruments around the circle, they will anticipate the action as soon as the educator stops the music and will be content to know that they will eventually have a turn using their instruments of choice. Those children using an instrument incorrectly respond well to having another child demonstrate the correct use and, in turn, that child enjoys the opportunity to help a friend.

I would like to add some thoughts on performances and concerts for the young child. Educators may feel a level of expectation from administrators, caregivers, or peer teachers to demonstrate the accomplishments of the children through recitals or performances. With children so young, their development of musical understanding cannot be measured by musicianship displayed during a performance. These children may not have the developmental maturity to perform, not to mention being observed by a large group of adults, and to deliver the expected behavior of such entertainment. It is possible to send home subjective evaluations regularly that focus on how much the child has advanced musically during the semester, or you might prefer to invite the caregivers or administrators to attend the music class and quietly observe the children's musical development, which will produce a much more accurate assessment. Most important, the children will continue to enjoy the music class without fear of judgment or expectations on the part of others.

Finally, each group of children will bring its own uniqueness to the classes, and what may work well with one group may not work with another. However, after the first few lessons, all in the class—including the educator—will become more comfortable with each other. Keeping a wide range of material to present, an open mind, a sense of humor, and flexible lesson plans will create wonderful opportunities for musical exploration for all.

The Educator

Considerable time and effort will bring the music class from initial conception to a blossoming, successful musical experience for all involved, and crucial to this success is the educator who provides the instruction. There are countless stories of incredible musical experiences evolving from some of the disadvantaged communities around the world and educators who have made significant contributions in less than ideal circumstances. A public speaker, church leader, salesperson, educator, or politician who speaks with confidence, passion, and knowledge of the subject at hand makes a great impact on his audience. Similarly, the effectiveness of the music instruction depends upon the educator's passion, knowledge, competence in the subject matter, and comfort level of his own musicianship.

The child's psychological safety demands that the overall environment instills a sense of belonging and well-being for each child, and the educator is the key to this success. Knowledge of child development and learning, the ability to communicate effectively with children and family, and demonstrating a caring, sensitive, and empathetic nature are critical characteristics for the educator. It is also important that the educator be able to understand and implement an effective program, use a variety of learning materials, and have the ability to reflect on his/her practice and make any appropriate changes.

The Mozart and the Young Mind curriculum provides the educator with every possible support and guidance to build confidence in the teaching of music and also provides the auditory tools upon which to develop musical skills. For those educators who are passionate about teaching music and have many years of experience, this program offers a fresh, new perspective with considerable flexibility to accommodate the educator's teaching style and the children's many learning styles.

Appendix B
ACTION SONGS

The Button and the Key

Around comes Scott, around comes he
He is hiding the button and the key
Who has the button? (*sung by the group*)
I have the button (*sung by the one child holding the button*)
Who has the key? (*sung by the group*)
I have the key (*sung by the one child holding the key*)

Children sit in a circle with their eyes closed and hands cupped behind their backs to receive a button or a key. While those sitting sing the song, one child walks around the outside of the circle, placing the button and the key in the cupped hands of two different children. This must be completed by the time the group finishes singing the words, "She is hiding the button and the key." Everyone sings, "Who has the button?" and then listens carefully to the one child who responds with, "I have the button." All sing, "Who has the key?" and once again listen carefully to the response trying to recognize the voice. Once the song is sung, the child on the outside of the circle calls on circle members who indicate that they have recognized the voices of those who sang and can identify them. Once identified correctly, that child takes the place of the child on the outside of the circle and now takes a turn placing the button and key in the cupped hands of two friends while the song is sung.

Hello

Hello, Hello, Hello
Ti tripleti trip ti trip
Good bye, Good bye, Good bye
Ti tripleti, tripleti, trip
Ti-tripleti, tripleti, triple (x3)
Ti-tripleti, tripleti, trip

Children find a partner and face each other to begin the song.

Line 1: Each child claps hands for the first syllable of "Hel-lo" and slaps his partner's hands (palms together) for the second syllable of "Hel-lo."
Line 2: Partners link right elbows and skip around, making a half circle turn, to trade places.
Line 3: Repeat the clap-slap movement for the words "good bye."
Line 4: Link left arms and go back to their original positions
Line 5: All children separate from their partners and skip around the room and take the closest child as a partner by the end of the song.

Now facing the new partner the song is once again repeated.

123

Open, Shut Them

Open, shut them, open, shut them
Give a little clap, clap, clap
Open, shut them, open, shut them
Lay them in your lap, tap
Creep them, creep them, creep them, creep them
Almost to your chin
Open wide your little mouth
Do not let them in.

Falling, falling, falling, falling
Almost to the ground
Quickly pick them up again
Gently lay them down
Roll them, roll them, roll them, roll them
Faster, faster, faster . . . .
Slowly, slowly, slowly, slowly
Gently lay them down.

Line 1. Open and shut hands as directed by text.
Line 2. Place palms of hands together and tap.
Line 4. Fold hands in lap and gently tap together.
Line 5. Walk fingers slowly up toward the chin.
Line 7. Open mouth wide, and wait.
Line 8. Quickly hide hands behind the back.
Line 9. Start with hands above the head and slowly let them fall just above the ground.
Line 11. Quickly lift hand above head.
Line 12. Fold hands in lap
Line 13. An exaggerated slow roly-poly movement with arms, becoming faster and faster.
Line 15. Gradually the roly-poly movement becomes slower and slower.
Line 16. Once again calmly fold hands in lap.

This song may be repeated in complete silence with just hand actions for added practice in inner hearing, timing, and rhythm.

Scotland's Burning

When introducing with solfège see below, when introducing with hand signs, refer to Curwen-Kodály hand signs. Start with the hand position for a low *so*; which is with arms outstretched facing downward and hands clapping together.

Scotland's burning, Scotland's burning   *Sol–sol–do–do, Sol–sol–do–do*
Look out, Look out,   *Re–mi, Re–mi*
Fire, fire, fire, fire   *Sol,* (clap hands above head) *sol–sol–sol*
Pour on water, pour on water,   *Sol–sol–do–do, Sol–sol–do–do*
(clap this *sol* as low—hands down together)

This song may be repeated in complete silence with just hand actions for added practice in inner hearing, timing, and rhythm.

Appendix C
TRACKS ON CDS BY LESSON PLAN

CD 1

SEPTEMBER

Lesson Plan 1: Introduce repertoire of songs.

1. "Bombalalom"
2. "Here We Are Together"
3. "Mary's Wearing Her Red Dress"
4. "Twinkle, Twinkle Little Star"
5. "Finger Song"
6. "Turn Around, Clap, Clap"
7. "Clap, Clap, Clap"
8. "Irish Jig"—loud and soft
9. "A Ram Sam Sam"
10. "Old MacDonald"
11. "Do Re Mi" (sitting)
12. "Open, Shut Them"

OCTOBER

Lesson Plan 2: Introduce solfège and hand signs beginning with **do**, **re**, *and then* **mi**.

13. "Bombalalom"
14. "Here We Are Together"
15. "Finger Song"
16. Farm animals—goat, sheep, donkey, horse
17. "If You're Happy and You Know It"
18. "Do, Re, Mi" (body movement)
19. "Do, Re"
20. "Do, Re, Mi"
21. Staccato and Legato
22. Mozart—"Twinkle, Twinkle"—high and low
23. "A Ram Sam Sam"
24. "Freight Train"—tempo
25. "I Hear the Mill Wheel"
26. "Open, Shut Them"

NOVEMBER

Lesson Plan 3: Explore musical styles through dance and movement with scarves.

27. "Bombalalom"
28. "Here We Are Together"
29. "I'm in the Mood for Clapping "
30. "Wake Up, Toes"
31. "Turn Around, Clap, Clap"
32. "A Ram Sam Sam"
33. Winter friends—coyote, chickadee, cardinal, squirrel
34. "Hot Cross Buns"
35. "Do You Know the Muffin Man?"
36. Beethoven, "Ode to Joy"—*freeze*
37. "Freight Train"
38. "Aiken Drum"
39. "Open, Shut Them"

DECEMBER

Lesson Plan 4: Introduce world cultures and customs.

40. "Bombalalom"
41. "Here We Are Together"
42. "Mary's Wearing Her Red Dress"
    Intro to percussion bells and shakers
41. "Do, Re, Mi"
42. "Do, Re"
43. "Do, Re, Mi"
44. Staccato and legato
45. Handel's *Messiah*—*dynamic expression*

JANUARY

Lesson Plan 5: Introduce percussion instruments (see lesson plans)

48. "Bombalalom"
49. "Here We Are Together"
50. "I'm in the Mood for Clapping"
51. "Wake Up, Toes"
52. "Clap, Clap, Clap"
53. "Do, Re, Mi"
54. "Do, Re"
55. "Do, Re, Mi"
56. Staccato and Legato
57. "Clickety, Clickety, Clack"
58. "Scotland's Burning"
59. "Going to Kentucky"
60. "Sakura"—*dance with scarves*
61. "Ragtime"

62. Animal sounds—goat, donkey, sheep, hors
63. "A Ram Sam Sam"
64. "I Hear the Mill Wheel"
65. "Freight Train"
66. "Toumba"—Israel
67. "Open, Shut Them"

CD 2

FEBRUARY

Lesson Plan 6: Timeline of composers

1. "Bombalalom"
2. "Clap, Clap, Clap"
3. "Row, Row, Row Your Boat"
4. "Do, Re, Mi"
5. "Do, Re"
6. "Do, Re, Mi"
7. Staccato and legato
8. "Scotland's Burning"
9. "Going to Kentucky"
10. Animal sounds—raccoon, robin, grasshopper, owl
11. Winter friends—coyote, chickadee, cardinal, squirrel
12. "I Hear the Mill Wheel"
13. "Toumba"; silence game
14. "Open, Shut Them"

MARCH

Lesson Plan 7: Introduce Prokofiev's **Peter and the Wolf,** *and follow with attendance to a live concert by the local orchestra or community band.*

March: Weeks 1 and 2

15. "Bombalalom"
16. "Here We Are Together"; Introduce half of *Peter and the Wolf* (10 minutes each day)
17. "Going to Kentucky"
18. "Scotland's Burning"
19. "Open, Shut Them"

March: Week 3

Peter and the Wolf: poster of characters and corresponding instruments
Review of instruments

March: Week 4

Peter and the Wolf: matching character cards and instrument cards
Introduction to orchestral families of instruments

APRIL

Lesson Plan 8: Introduce mapping of song, timbre recognition, and staff notation

20. "Hello"
     Solfège
21. "Scotland's Burning"
22. Baby animals—kittens, ducklings, puppies, baby birds
23. Spring sounds—raccoon, robin, grasshopper, owl
24. "The Button and the Key"
25. "Row, Row, Row Your Boat"—*mapping*
26. "Bombalalom"—*mapping*
27. "Open, Shut Them"

MAY

Lesson Plan 9: Notation on the staff and dynamic cards

28. "Hello"
29. "Down by the Bay"
30. "Scotland's Burning"
31. Gershwin—jazz/ragtime
32. "Row, Row, Row Your Boat"

References

Adams, M. J. (1990). *Beginning to read: Thinking and learning about print.* Cambridge, MA: MIT Press.

Andersson, B. E. (1989). The importance of public day care for preschool children's later development. *Child Development, 60*(4), 857–66.

Aronoff, F. W. (1979). *Music and young children: Expanded edition.* New York: Turning Wheel Press.

Ashton, P. T. & Webb, R. B. (1986). *Making a difference: Teachers' sense of efficacy, and student achievement.* New York: Longman.

Bachmann, M. L. (1991). *Dalcroze today: An education through and into music.* New York: Oxford University Press.

Balkwill, L. L., Thompson, W. F., & Matsunaga, R. (2004). Recognition of emotion in Japanese, Western, and Hindustani music by Japanese listeners. *Japanese Psychological Research, 46*(4), 337–49.

Balodis, F. (1995). Music for Young Children. *A Program for Children of All Ages Who Want to Learn Music and Have Fun Doing It* (self-published brochure). An informative brochure detailing this child-centered approach to learning music.

Begley, S. (1997). How to build a baby's brain. *Newsweek* (Spring/Summer), 28–32.

Belsky, J. & MacKinnon, C. (1994). Transition to school: Developmental trajectories and school experiences. *Early Education and Development, 5*(2), 106–19.

Bennett, P. G. (1992). Perspectives: On preparing classroom teachers to teach music. *Journal of Music Teacher Education, 1*, 22–27.

Berk, L. (2004). *Developing through the lifespan* (3rd ed.). New York: Allyn & Bacon.

Best, A. B. (1991). *Teaching children with visual impairments.* Milton Keynes, PA: Open University Press.

Blacking, J. (1973). *How musical is man?* Seattle: University of Washington Press.

Blacking, J. (1995). *Venda children's songs.* Chicago: University of Chicago Press.

Boehnlein, M. M. (1990). Research and evaluation summary of Montessori programs. In D. Kahn (ed.), *Implementing Montessori education in the public sector* (pp. 476–83). Cleveland, OH: The North American Montessori Teachers' Association.

Boehnlein, M. M. (1998). Montessori research analysis in retrospect. *The North American Montessori Teachers' Association Journal, 13*(3), 1–119.

Boudreau, D. M. & Hedberg, N. L. (1999). A comparison of early literacy skills in children with specific language impairment and their typically developing peers. *American Journal of Speech-Language Pathology, 8*, 249–60.

Boyce-Tillman, J. (2007). Spirituality in early childhood music education. In K. Smithrim & R. Upitis (eds.), *Listen to their voices: Research and practice in early childhood music.* Toronto, ON: Canadian Music Educators Association.

Bredekamp, S. (1987). *Developmentally appropriate practice in early childhood programs serving children from birth through age eight.* Washington, DC: National Association for the Education of Young Children.

Bresler, L. (1994). Music in a double bind: Instruction by non-specialists in elementary schools. *Arts Education Policy Review, 95*(3), 30–36.

Brody, J. (1991). Not just music, bird song is a means of courtship and defense. *New York Times,* April 9.

Buchen, I., Milley, J., Oderlund, A., & Mortarotti, J. (1983). *The arts: An essential ingredient in education.* San Francisco: California Council of the Fine Arts Deans.

Bunt, L. (1994). *Music therapy: An art beyond words.* London: Routledge.

Burt, L., Holm, A., & Dodd, B. (1999). Phonological awareness skills of four year old British children: An assessment and developmental data. *International Journal of Language and Communication Disorders, 34*(3), 311–35.

Burton, J., Horowitz, R., & Abeles, H. (1999). *Learning in and through the arts: Curriculum implications.* Washington, DC: Arts Education Partnership and the President's Committee on the Arts and Humanities.

Butzlaff, R. (2000). Can music be used to teach reading? *Journal of Aesthetic Education, 34*(3–4), 167–78.

Campbell, D. (1997). *The Mozart effect.* New York: Avon Books.

Campbell, P. S. (1998). *Songs in their heads: Music and its meaning in children's lives.* New York: Oxford University Press.

Carstens, C., Huskins, E., & Hounshell, G. (1995). Listening to Mozart may not enhance performance on the revised Minnesota paper form board test. *Psychological Reports 77*(1), 111–14.

Catterall, J. (1998). Does experience in the arts boost academic achievement? *Art Education, 51*(3), 6–11.

Catterall, J., Chapleau, R., & Iwanaga, J. (1999). *Involvement in the arts and human development: General involvement and intensive involvement in music and theater arts* [Internet]. University of California. Retrieved July 15, 2005, from http://www.aep-arts.org/highlights/resources/toolkits/criticallinks.impacts.doc.

Children's Center for the Visually Impaired, (n.d.). Programs & Services Overview. Retrieved July 29, 2008, from http://www.trolleyrun.org/programs_and_services.asp

Choksy, L. (1974). *The Kodaly Method: Comprehensive music education from infant to adult.* Englewood Cliffs, NJ: Prentice-Hall, Inc.

Choksy, L. (1999). *The Kodaly Method: Comprehensive music education from infant to adult.* Englewood Cliffs, NJ: Prentice Hall, Inc.

Choksy, L., Abramson, R. M., Gillespie, A., & Woods, D. (1986). *Teaching music in the twentieth century.* Englewood Cliffs, NJ: Prentice Hall.

Choksy, L., Abramson, R. M., Gillespie, A., & Woods, D. (2000). *Teaching music in the twentieth century* (2nd ed.). New Jersey: Prentice Hall.

Clark, C. & Akerman, R. (2006). *Social inclusion and reading: An exploration.* London: National Literacy Trust.

Clifford, A. J. & Takacs, C. (1991). Marotta Montessori schools of Cleveland follow-up study of urban center pupils. Unpublished manuscript, Cleveland State University, Cleveland, Ohio.

Clough, L. (2004, June 16–20). *Finding a voice: Case study of music therapy with a young selective communicator/mute from an asylum seeker background.* Unpublished presentation to the 6th European Music Therapy Congress, University of Jyvaskyla, Finland.

Cobb, P., Yackel, E., & Wood, T. (1992). A constructivist alternative to the representational view of mind in mathematics education. *Journal for Research in Mathematics Education, 23*(1), 2–33.

Curtis, S. L. (1986). The effect of music on pain relief and relaxation of the terminally ill. *Journal of Music Therapy, 23*, 10–24.

Daignault, L. (1996). *Children's creative musical thinking within the context of a computer-supported improvisational approach to composition.* (Doctoral Dissertation, Northwestern University). *Dissertation Abstracts International, 57*, 4681A.

D'Amato, M. (1988). A search for tonal pattern perception in Cebus monkeys: Why monkeys can't hum a tune. *Music Perception 5*(4), 453–80.

Dean, J. & Gross, I. L. (1992). Teaching basic skills through art and music. *Phi Delta Kappan, 73*(8), 613–18.

DeBedout, J. K. & Worden, M. C. (2006). Motivators for children with severe intellectual disabilities in the self-contained classroom: A movement analysis. *Journal of Music Therapy, 43*(2), 123–35.

DeCasper, A. J. & Fifer, W. (1980). Of human bonding: Newborns prefer their mothers' voices. *Science, 208*(4448), 1174–76.

Dewey, J. (1934). *Art as experience.* New York: Putnam.

Dewey, J. (1966). *Democracy and education: An introduction to the philosophy of education.* New York: Free Press.

Dewey, J. (1980). *Art as experience.* New York: Perigree Books.

DiPietro, J. (2000). Baby and the brain: Advances in child development. *Annual Review of Public Health 21*, 455–71.

Duax, T. (1989). Preliminary report on the educational effectiveness of a Montessori school in the public sector. *North American Teachers' Association Journal, 14*(2), 56–62.

Edgerton, C. L. (1994). The effect of improvisational music therapy on the communicative behaviors of autistic children. *Journal of Music Therapy, 31*, 31–62.

Eisler, R. (1987). *The chalice and the blade: Our history, our future.* San Francisco: Harper & Row.

Eisner, E. W. (1994). *Cognition and curriculum reconsidered* (2nd ed.). New York: Teachers College Press.

Elliott, S. N., Argulewicz, E. N., & Turco, T. L. (1986). Predictive validity of the scales for rating the behavioral characteristics of superior students for gifted children from three sociocultural groups. *Journal of Experimental Education, 55*(1), 27–32.

Entwisle, D. R., Alexander, K. L., Cadigan, D., & Pallas, A. (1986). The schooling process in first grade: Two samples a decade apart. *American Educational Research Journal, 23*(4), 587–613.

Evans, E. D. & Tribble, M. (1986). Perceived teaching problems, self-efficacy, and commitment to teaching among preservice teachers. *Journal of Educational Research, 80*(2), 81–85.

Falk, C. (2004). Hmong instructions to the dead: What the qeej say in the Qeej Tu Siav. Part 1. *Asian Folklore* Studies 63(1), 1–29.

Falk, D. (2000). Hominid brain evolution and the origins of music. In N. L. Wallen, B. Merker, & S. Brown (eds.), *The origins of music* (pp. 197–216). Cambridge, MA: The MIT Press.

Feierabend, J. (1997). Music and movement for infants and toddlers: Naturally wonder-full. *Kodaly Enjoy 23*(2), 7–10.

Ficken, T. (1976). The use of songwriting in a psychiatric setting. *Journal of Music Therapy, 13*(4), 163–72.

Finnerty, J. (1999). From lizards to Picasso: The application of neurological research. Paper presented at the Learning and the Brain Conference, Boston, MA.

Fisher, A. (2002). *Radical ecopsychology: Psychology in the service of life.* New York: SUNY Press.

Flohr, J. E., Persellin, D. C., Miller, D. C. (1993). Quantitative EEG Differences between baseline and psychomotor response to music. *Texas Music Education Research, 1*–7.

Flohr, J. W., Persellin, D. C., & Miller, D. C. (1996). *Children's electro physical responses to music.* Paper presented at the 22nd International Society for Music Education World Conference, Amsterdam, Netherlands, July.

Frazee, J. & Kreuter, K. (1987). *Discovering Orff: A curriculum for music teachers.* New York: Schott Music Corporation.

Freire, P. (1973). *Education for critical conscientious continuum.* New York: Continuum International Publishing Group.

Gagne, F. (2003). Transforming gifts into talents: The DMGT as a developmental theory. In N. Colangelo & G. A. Davis (eds.), *Handbook on gifted education* (3rd ed.), (pp. 60–74). Boston, MA: Allyn and Bacon.

Gallahue, D. L. (1982). *Understanding motor development in children.* New York: John Wiley & Sons.

Galliford, J. (2006). The effects of experience during early childhood on the development of linguistic and non-linguistic skills. Unpublished paper presented at the MENC conference, April, Salt Lake City, Utah.

Gamlin, P. J. & Luther, M. G. (1993). Dynamic assessment approaches with young children and adolescents. *International Journal of Cognitive Education and Mediated Learning, 2*(1), 25–41.

Gardiner, M., Fox, A., Knowles, F., & Jeffrey, D. (1996). Learning improved by arts training. *Nature, 381*(6580), 284–85.

Gardner, H. (1973). *The arts and human development: A psychological study of the artistic process.* New York: Wiley & Sons.

Gardner, H. (1983). *Frames of mind: Theory of multiple intelligences.* New York: HarperCollins.

Gardner, H. (1999a). The disciplined mind: Beyond facts and standardized tests, the K–12 education that every child deserves. New York: Penguin Putnam.

Gardner, H. (1999b). *Intelligence reframed: Multiple intelligences for the 21st century.* New York: Basic Books.

Gelman, R., & Brown, A. L. (1986). Changing views of cognitive competence in the young. In N. Smelser & D. Gerstein (eds.), *Discoveries and trends in behavioral and social science* (pp. 175–207). Washington, DC: National Academic Press.

Geoghegan, N., & Mitchelmore, M. (1996). Possible effects of early childhood music on mathematical achievement. *Australian Research in Early Childhood, 1,* 57–64.

George, A. E. (1912). *The Montessori method.* New York: Frederick A. Stokes Co.

Gestwicki, C. (1999). *Developmentally appropriate practice: Curriculum and development in early education.* New York: Delmar Publishers.

Gibson, F. J. (1969). *Principles and perceptional learning and development.* New York: Appleton-Century-Crofts.

Gibson, S. & Dembo, M. H. (1984). Teacher efficacy: A construct validation. *Journal of Educational Psychology, 76*(4), 569–82.

Gilbert, J. P. (1979). Assessment of motor skill development in young children: Test construction and evaluation procedures. *Psychology of Music, 7*(2), 21–25.

Gilman L. & Paperte, F. (1952). Music as a psychotherapeutic agent. In E. A. Gutheil (ed.), *Music and your emotions* (pp. 24–55). New York: Liveright Publishing Co.

Ginsburg, H. P. & Baroody A. J. (2003). *Test of early math ability* (3rd ed.). Texas: PRO-ED.

Glassman, L. R. (1991). Music therapy and bibliotherapy in the rehabilitation of traumatic brain injury: A case study. *Arts in Psychotherapy, 18*(2), 149–56.

Golden, D. (1994). Building a better brain. *Life* (July), 62–70.

Gordon, E. E. (1995). *Jump right in: The instrumental series.* [Recorded by Grunow, R. F., Gordon, E. E., & Azzara, C. D.] Chicago, IL: GIA Publications.

Gordon, E. E. (1997). *A music learning theory for newborn and young children* (2nd Ed.). Chicago: GIA Publications.

Gordon, E. E. (2003). *A music learning theory for newborn and young children.* Chicago: GIA Publications.

Gordon, E. E., Bolton, B. M., Reynolds, A. M., Taggart, & C. C., Valerio, W. H. (1998). *Music play: The early childhood music curriculum.* Chicago, IL: GIA Publications.

Green, R. (1947). The music program in Veterans Administration Hospitals. *National Music Council Bulletin, 7,* 20–21.

Green, R. (1948). Music in Veterans Administration hospitals. *National Music Council Bulletin, 8,* 15–17.

Green, R. (1950). Veterans Administration hospital music. *Hospital Music Newsletter, 2,* 22–23.

Greene, M. (1995). *Releasing the imagination.* San Francisco. CA: Jossey-Bass Inc.

Gromko, J. E., (2005). The effect of music instruction on phonemic awareness in beginning readers. *Journal of Research in Music Education, 53*(3), 199–209.

Gruhn, W., Altenmuller, E., & Babler, R. (1997). The influence of learning on cortical activation patterns. *Bulletin of the Council for Research in Music Education, 133*(2), 25–30.

Guilford, J. P. (1968). *Intelligence, creativity and their educational implications.* San Diego: Robert R. Knapp.

Guilmartin, K. K. (2002). Ages and stages: Is that the same child I taught last year? The very young child. *American Music Teacher, 52*(2), 26–28.

Guskey, T. R. (1988). Teacher efficacy, self-concept, and attitudes toward the implementation of instructional innovation. *Teaching and Teacher Education, 4*(1), 63–69.

Hainstock, E. G. (1997). *The essential Montessori: An introduction to the woman, the writings, the method, and the movement* (3rd ed.). New York: Penguin Books.

Halliday, M. A. K. (1977). *Explorations in the functions of language.* New York: Elsevier North-Holland.

Hargreaves, D. J. (1994). Musical educational for all. *Psychologist, 7,* 357–358.

Hargreaves, D. J., & Davis, M. A. (2000). Learning . . . the beat goes on. *Childhood Education, 76*(3), 148–54.

Harris, M. A. (2004). *Montessori Mozarts make music.* Unpublished Handbook for Teachers.

Harris, M. A. (2005a). *Differences in mathematics scores between students who received traditional Montessori instruction and students who received enriched Montessori instruction.* (Unpublished master's dissertation, University of Windsor, Ontario, Canada.)

Harris, M. A. (2005b). Montessori Mozart programme. *Montessori International Journal, 75,* 17.

Harris, M. A. (2005c). Montessori research. *Montessori International Journal, 76,* 54.

Harris, M. A. (2006). *The effects of music-enriched instruction on the mathematics scores of pre-school children.* Bridges London, Mathematics, Music, Art, Architecture, Culture Conference proceedings, 2006. http://www.sckans.edu/~bridges/. Mathartfun.com, Taruin Books, UK.

Harris, M. A. (2007). Montessori, music, and math. In K. Smithrim & R. Upitis (eds.), *Listen to their voices: Research and practice in early childhood music* (pp. 243–53). Toronto, ON: Canadian Music Educators Association.

Harris, M. (2007). Montessori, music and math. In Upitis, R., & Smithrim, K. (eds.) *Listen to their Voices: Research to Practice*, Vol. 3. Toronto: Canadian Music Educators Association. **[AU2]**

Hepper, P. G. (1991). An examination of fetal learning before and after birth. *Irish Journal of Psychology, 12*, 95–107.

Hickerson, M. (1983). *A comparison of left and right brain hemisphere processing and brain related sex differences in kindergarten children.* (Unpublished doctoral dissertation, East Tennessee State University). *Dissertation Abstracts International 44/05*, 1388, (UMI 8315321).

Himes, D. (2004, June). *Dalcroze Eurythmics: Living the music.* Paper presented at the Royal Conservatory of Music, Toronto, ON.

Hodges, D. A. (1996). Human musicality. In D. A. Hodges (ed.), *Handbook of music psychology* (pp. 29–68). San Antonio, TX: IMR Press.

Hodges, D. (2000). *Why are we musical? Support for an evolutionary theory on human musicality.* Paper presented at the 6th International Conference on Music Perception and Cognition, Keele, England.

Hoermann, D. B. (1974). The role of the elementary classroom teacher in music education. *ISME Yearbook (Challenges in Music Education), XI Perth*, 128–34.

Hoffman, J. (1997, June). Tuning in to the power of music. *RN, 60*, 52–54.

Hoffman, J. (2003). Music, math and the mind. *Today's Parent.* Retrieved October 8, 2004, from http://www.todaysparent.com/education/general/article.

Hurwitz, I., Wolff, P. H., Bortnick, B. D., & Kokas, K. (1975). Nonmusical effects of the Kodaly music curriculum in primary grade children. *Journal of Learning Disabilities, 8*, 45–51.

Husain, G., Thompson, W. F., & Schellenberg, E. G. (2002). Effects of musical tempo and mode on arousal, mood, and spatial abilities. *Music Perception, 20*(2), 151–71.

Jackson, N. A. (2003, Winter). A survey of music therapy methods and their role in the treatment of early elementary school children with ADHD. *Journal of Music Therapy, 40* (4).

Jellison, J. A. (2000). A content analysis of music research with disabled children and youth (1975–1999): Applications in special education. In American Music Therapy Association (eds.), *Effectiveness of music therapy procedures: Documentation of research and clinical practice* (pp. 199–264). Silver Spring, MD: AMTA.

Jensen, E. (2001). *Arts with the brain in mind.* Alexandria, VA: Association for Supervision and Curriculum Development.

Kaempffert, W. (1944, April 16). Science in review: Possibilities of music in aiding the mentally ill will be tested at Soldier's Hospital. *The New York Times*, p. E9.

Kalmar, M., (1989). The effects of music education on the acquisition of some attribute-concepts in preschool children. *Canadian Music Educator, 30*(2), 5–59.

Kandel, E. R., Schwartz, J. H., & Jessell, T. M. (2000). *Principles of neural science* (4th ed.). New York: McGraw-Hill.

Katz, L. (1993). *Dispositions as educational goals.* ERIC Digest (Report No. EPO-PS-93–10). Retrieved from ERIC database.

Kelstrom, J. M. (1998). The untapped power of music: Its role in the curriculum and its effect on academic achievement. *NASSP Bulletin, 82*, 34–43.

Kelly, S. N. (1998). Preschool classroom teachers' perceptions of useful music skills and understandings. *Journal of Research in Music Education, 46*(3), 374–83.

Kern, P. & Wolery, M. (2001). Participation of a preschooler with visual impairments on the playground: Effects of musical adaptations and staff development. *Journal of Music Therapy, 38*(2), 149–64.

Kindermusik Foundations of Learning. (2001). *Put your life to music.* Retrieved July 29, 2008, from http://www.kindermusik.com/Teach/KI_Brochures/KIBrochureFront.htm

Kirchner, F. (1998, January 14). *Governor wants to soothe Georgia newborns with classical tunes*, Press release, Atlanta Associated Press.

Klinger, R. (1996, Fall). Children's song acquisition: Learning through immersion. *Orff Echo, 29*(1), 35–36.

Koen, B. D. (2005). Medical ethnomusicology in the Pamir Mountains: Music and prayer in healing. *Journal of Ethnomusicology, 49*(2), 287–311.

Kolb, G. R. (1996). Reading with a beat: Developing literacy through music and song. *The Reading Teacher, 50*(1), 76–79.

La Fontaine, J. (1990). *Child sexual abuse.* Cambridge, UK: Polity Press.

Lamb, S. J. & Gregory, A. H. (1993). The relationship between music and reading in beginning readers. *Educational Psychology, 13*, 19–27.

Leach, P. (1994). *Children first.* New York: Alfred A. Knopf.

Lecanuet, J. P. (1996). Prenatal auditory experience. In I. Deliege and J. Sloboda (eds.). *Musical beginnings* (pp. 3–34). Oxford: Oxford University Press.

Lee, D. J., Chen, Y., & Schlaug, G. (2003). Corpus callosum: Musician and gender effects. *NeuroReport, 14*(2), 205–9.

Lehrman, P. D. (2007). The healing power of music. *Mix*, 31(5).

Lemonick, M. (2000). *Music on the brain: Biologists and psychologists join forces to investigate how and why humans appreciate music.* OH: Glencoe/McGraw-Hill.

Levine, M. (2002). *A mind at a time.* New York: Simon & Schuster.

Liu, H., Kuhl, P., & Tsao, F. (2003). An association between mothers' speech clarity and infants' speech discrimination skills. *Developmental Science 6*(3): 1–10.

Marsh, A. (1999). Can you hum your way to math genius? *Forbes, 16*: 176–80.

McKay, L. A. (1945). Music as a group therapeutic agent in the treatment of convalescents. *Sociometry, 8*(3/4), 233–37.

McPherson, G. E. (2005). From child to musician: Skill development during the beginning stages of learning an instrument. *Psychology of Music, 33*(1), 5–35.

Megel, M. E., Houser, C. W., & Gleaves, L. S. (1998). Children's responses to immunizations: Lullabies as a distraction. *Issues in Comprehensive Pediatric Nursing, 21*(3), 129–45.

Mickela, T. (1990). Does music have an impact on the development of students? A paper presented at the California Music Educators State Convention.

Miller, J. K. (1999). *Montessori music: Sensorial exploration and notation with the bells.* California: Nienhaus Montessori.

Milley, J., Buchen, I., Oderlund, A., & Mortatotti, J. (1983). *The arts: An essential ingredient in education.* Mountain View, CA: California Council of Fine Arts Deans.

Mitchell, N. (Host). (2007, May 5). *All in the mind: Is music the universal language?* [Radio broadcast]. Melbourne: ABC Radio National.

Montessori, M. (1899). *To educate the human potential* (The Clio Montessori Series). Oxford, UK: ABC-CLIO.

Montessori, M. (1964). *The Montessori method.* New York: Schocken Books.

Moore, D. G., Burland, K., & Davidson, J. W. (2003). The social context of musical success: A developmental account. *British Journal of Psychology, 94*(4), 529–49.

Morgan, S. (1978). A comparative assessment of some aspects of number and arithmetical skills in Montessori and traditional preschools. Unpublished doctoral dissertation, Syracuse University, New York.

Morton, L. L., Kershner, J. R., & Siegel, L. S. (1990). The potential for therapeutic applications of music on problems related to memory and attention. *Journal of Music Therapy, 4*, 195–208.

Mrazek, P. B. & Kempe, C. H. (1981). *Sexually abused children and their families.* Oxford: Pergamon Press.

Nash, M. J. (1997). Fertile minds. *Time* (Feb. 3).

National Association for the Education of Young Children (1997). Early Intervention Programs, retrieved from http://www.naeyc.org/about/positions/pdf/PSDAP98.PDF.

National Association for the Education of Young Children (2001a). *Guidelines for preparation of early childhood professionals*, retrieved from http://www. naeyc.org/faculty/college.asp.

National Association for the Education of Young Children (2001b). *Top 10 signs of a good kindergarten classroom.* Retrieved May 6, 2004, from http://www.naeyc.org/ece/1996/12.asp

National Association for the Education of Young Children (2004, March). Suggested starter equipment for movement curriculums, Beyond the Journal, *Young Children* on the Web. Retrieved July 29, 2008, from http://www.journal.naeyc.org/btj/200403/PhysicalActivity Fitness.pdf

National Association for Sport and Physical Education (2004). *Moving into the future: National standards for physical education*, (2nd ed.). National Standards for Physical Education. New York: McGraw-Hill.

National Reading Panel. (2000). *Report: Teaching children to read.* National Institute of Child Health and Human Development (NIH Publication 00–4769), Washington, DC: Government Printing Office. Retrieved on November 14, 2006, from www.nich.nih.gov/publication/nrp/smallbrook.

New South Wales Board of Studies (1994). *Otitis media and Aboriginal children: A handbook for teachers and communities.* Sydney, Australia: Board of Studies.

New South Wales Board of Studies (1995). *Outcomes statements and pointers: English K–10, draft for consultation.* Sydney, Australia: Board of Studies.

New York City Board of Education. (1980). *Learning to read through the arts, title I children's program.* New York: Division of Curriculum and Instruction, Board of Education.

Nietzsche, F. (1888). *Twilight of the idols.* "Maxims and Arrows," #33. Retrieved April 8, 2008, from http://en.wikiquote.org/wiki/Friedrich_Nietzsche#Twilight_of_the_Idols_.281888.29

Nocker-Ribaupierre, M. (1999). Premature birth and music therapy. In T. Wigram & J. De Backer (eds.), *Clinical applications of music therapy in developmental disability, paediatrics and neurology* (pp. 47–65). London: Jessica Kingsley Publishers.

Noguchi, L. K. (2006). The effect of music versus non-music on behavioral signs of distress and self-report of pain in pediatric injection patients. *Journal of Music Therapy, 43*(1), 16–38.

Nye, V. T. (1983). *Music for young children* (3rd ed.). Dubuque, IA: William C. Brown Co.

Oddleifson, E. (1990). *Music education as a gateway to improved academic performance in reading, math, and science.* Washington, DC: Center for Arts in the Basic Curriculum.

O'Herron, P. & Siebenaler, D. (2006). *The intersection between vocal music and language arts instruction: A review of the literature.* Unpublished dissertation, California State University, Fullerton CA.

Olsho, L. (1984). Infant frequency discrimination. *Infant Behavior and Development, 7*, 27–35.

Ostrandra, S., & Schroeder, L. (1979). *Superlearning.* New York: Delacorte Press, 1979.

Papousek, H. (1996). Musicality in infancy research: Biological and cultural origins of early musicality. In I. Deliege & J. Sloboda (eds.), *Musical beginnings: Origins and development of musical competence* (pp. 37–55). New York: Oxford.

Papousek, M. (1994). Melodies in care givers' speech: A species-specific guidance toward language. *Early Development and Parenting, 3*(1), 5–17.

Papousek, M. & Papousek, H. (1981). Musical elements in the infant's vocalizations: Their significance for communication cognition and creativity. *Advances in Infancy Research, 1,* 163–224.

Patel, A., Iversen, J., & Ohgushi, K. (2004). Cultural differences in rhythm perception: What is the influence of native language? *Proceedings of the 8th International Conference on Music Perception and Cognition,* Evanston, IL: Northwestern University CD-ROM.

Patel, A. (1998). Syntactic processing in language and music: Different cognitive operations, similar neural resources? *Music Perception, 16*(1), 27–42.

Patel, A. D. (2003a). Language, music, syntax and the brain. *Nature Neuroscience, 6*(7), 674–81.

Patel, A. D. (2003b). Rhythm in language and music: Parallels and differences. *Annals of the New York Academy of Sciences, 99,* 140–43.

Patterson, A. (2003). Music teachers and music therapists: Helping children together. *Music Educators Journal, 89*(4), 35–38.

Perry, B. D. (2000). The developmental hot zone. *Early Childhood Today 15*(3), 30–32.

Perry, B. D., Pollard, R. A., Blakley, T. L., Baker, W. L., & Vigilante, D. (1995). Childhood trauma, the neurobiology of adaptation, and 'use dependent' development of the brain: How 'states' become 'traits.' *Infant Mental Health Journal, 16*(4), 271–91.

Persellin, D. (2000). The effect of activity-based music instruction on spatial-temporal task performance of young children. *Early Childhood Connections* (Fall), 21–29.

Pestalozzi, J. H. (1976). *Leonard and Gertrude.* New York: Gordon Press Publishers.

Piaget, J. (1951). *Play, dreams, and imitation in childhood.* New York: W. W. Norton.

Plato, Jowett, B., & Bulkley, C. H. A. (1883). *Plato's Best Thoughts,* New York: Charles Scribner's Sons, retrieved July 21, 2008, from http://books.google.com/books?id=3H7ts8406g4C&printsec=frontcover&dq=Plato%27s+best+thoughts

Plude, D. J., Enns, J. T., & Brodeur, D. (1994). The development of selective attention: A life-span overview. *Acta Psychologica, 86*(2/3), 227–72.

Pross, C. (2001). At the side of torture survivors: Treating a terrible assault on human dignity. *New England Journal of Medicine, 17*(345), 1284–85.

Raebeck, L. & Wheeler, L. (1972). *Orff and Kodaly adapted for the elementary school.* Dubuque, IA: William C. Brown Co.

Rathunde, K. (2001). Montessori education and optimal experience: A framework for new research. *North American Montessori Teachers' Association Journal, 26*(1), 11–43.

Rathunde, K. & Csikszentmihalyi, M. (2003). A comparison of Montessori and traditional middle schools: Motivation, quality of experience, and social context. *North American Montessori Teachers' Association Journal, 28*(3), 12–52.

Rauscher, F. (2004). Can (and should) current music education research influence music education? In S. D. Lipscomb, R. Ashely, R. O. Gjerdingern, & P. Webster (eds.), *Proceedings of the International Conference of Music Perception and Cognition, 8,* 119–21.

Rauscher, F., & Shaw, G. (1998). Key components of the Mozart effect. *Perceptual and Motor Skills, 86,* 835–41.

Rauscher, F., Shaw, G. L., & Ky, K. (1995). Listening to Mozart enhances spatial-temporal reasoning: Towards a neurophysiological basis. *Neuroscience Letters, 185,* 44–47.

Rauscher, F., Shaw, G. L., Levine, L., Wright, E., Dennis, W., & Newcomb, R. (1997). Music training causes long-term enhancement of preschool children's spatial-temporal reasoning. *Neurological Research, 19,* 2–8.

Rauscher, F. H., & Zupan, M. A. (2000). Classroom keyboard instruction improves kindergarten children's spatial-temporal performance. A field experiment. *Early Childhood Research Quarterly, 15*(2), 215–28.

Register, D. (2001). The effects of an early intervention music curriculum on prereading/writing. *Journal of Music Therapy, 38*(3), 239–48.

Register, D. (2004, Spring). The effects of live music groups versus an educational children's television program on the emergent literacy of young children. *The Journal of Music Therapy, 41*(1).

Reiner, R. (1997). *I am your child: The first years last forever,* hosted by Rob Reiner (Director) & the Reiner Foundation (Producer). (1997). *I am your child: The first years last forever* [VHS Tape]. Washington, DC: The Reiner Foundation.

Reinhardt, D. A. (1990, Fall). Preschool children's use of rhythm in improvisation. *Contributions to Music Education, 17,* 7–19.

Renzulli, J. S. (1986). The three-ring conception of giftedness: A developmental model for creative productivity. In R. J. Sternberg & J. Davidson (eds.), *Conceptions of giftedness* (pp. 53–92). New York: Cambridge University Press.

Richards, M. H. (1977). *Aesthetic foundations for thinking—rethought: Part 1 experience.* California: Richards Institute of Education Through Music.

Richards, M. H. (1978). *Aesthetic foundations for thinking—Reflection: Part 2.*

Robarts, J. Z. & Sloboda, J. A. (1994). Perspectives on music therapy with people suffering from anorexia nervosa. *Journal of British Music Therapy, 8*(1), 7–15.

Robb, S. L. (2003). Music interventions and group participation skills of preschoolers with visual impairments: Raising questions about music, arousal, and attention. *Journal of Music Therapy, 40*(4), 266–82.

Rockwell, J. (1974). *Fact in fiction: The use of literature in the systemic study of society.* London: Routledge & Kegan Paul.

Roehmann, F. L., & Wilson, F. R. (1988). *The biology of music making: Proceedings of the 1984 Denver conference.* St. Louis, MO: MMB Music Inc.

Rorke, M. A. (1996). Music and the wounded of World War II. *Journal of Music Therapy, 33* (Fall), 189–207.

Ross, J. A. (1992). Teacher efficacy and the effects of coaching on student achievement. *Canadian Journal of Education, 17*(1), 51–65.

Salas, J. & Gonzalez, D. (1991). Like singing with a bird: Improvisational music therapy with a blind four-year-old. In K. E. Bruscia (ed.), *Case studies in music therapy* (pp. 18–27). Gilsum, NH: Barcelona Publishers.

Saunders, T. C. & Baker, D. S. (1991). In-service classroom teachers' perceptions of useful music skills and understandings. *Journal of Research in Music Education, 39*(3), 248–61.

Schiller, W. & Veale, A. (1996). The arts: The real business of education. In W. Schiller (ed.), *Issues in expressive arts: Curriculum for early childhood* (pp. 5–14). Amsterdam, Holland: Gordon and Breach.

Schlaug, G. (1999). *Turning up the brain: Music and intellect.* Paper presented at the Learning and the Brain Conference, Boston, MA.

Schwartz, J. M., & Begley, S. (2002). *The mind & the brain: Neuroplasticity and the power of mental force.* New York: Regan Books.

Shore, R. (1997). *Rethinking the brain: New insights into early development.* New York: Families and Work Institute.

Simon, W. (1945). The value of music in resocialization and rehabilitation of the mentally ill. *Military Surgeon, 97,* 498–500.

Slavin, R. E., Madden, N. A., Dolan, L. J., & Wasik, B. A. (1996). Roots & wings: Universal excellence in elementary education. In S. Stringfield, S. Ross, & L. Smith (eds.), *Bold plans for school restructuring: The New American Shools Designs.* Mahwah, NJ: Lawrence Erlbaum Associates.

Sloboda, J. (1985). *The musical mind: The cognitive psychology of music.* Oxford: Clarendon Press.

Sloboda, J. A. (2001). *Emotion, functionality and the everyday experience of music: Where does music education fit?* Paper presented at the International Research in Music Education Conference, England.

Sloboda, J. A. & Davidson, J. W. (1996). The young performing musician. In I. Deliege & J. A. Sloboda (eds.), *Musical beginnings: The origins and development of musical competence* (pp. 171–90). London: Oxford University Press.

Sloboda, J. A. & Howe, M. J. A. (1991). Biographical precursors of musical excellence: An interview study. *Psychology of Music, 19*(1), 3–21.

Smee, E. (2004). *Kodály method: From infants to adults.* A paper presented at a Kodály workshop at the Royal Conservatory of Music, Toronto, Canada.

Smithrim, K., & Upitis, R. (2001). *Learning through the arts, national assessment, a report on year one.* Unpublished manuscript, Queens' University, Kingston, ON.

Solomon, M. (1995). *Mozart: A life.* New York: HarperCollins Publishers.

Soodak, L. C. & Podell, D. M. (1993). Teacher efficacy and student problem as factors in special education referral. *Journal of Special Education, 27*(1), 66–81.

Standley, J. M. & Hughes, J. E. (1997). Evaluation of an early intervention music curriculum for enhancing pre-reading/writing skills. *Music Therapy Perspectives, 15*(2), 79–86.

Stein, B. L., Hardy, C. A., & Totten, H. (1982). The use of music and imagery to enhance and accelerate information retention. *Journal of the Society for Accelerative Learning & Teaching, 7,* (4).

Sutton, J. P. (2002). *Music, music therapy and trauma: International perspectives.* London: Jessica Kingsley Publishers.

Sutton-Smith, B. (1997). *The ambiguity of play.* Cambridge, MA: Harvard University Press.

Suzuki, S. (1983). *Nurtured by love: The classic approach to talent education.* Smithtown, NY: Exposition Press.

Suzuki, S. & Mills, E. (1973). *The Suzuki concept: An introduction to a successful method for early music education.* Berkeley, CA: Diablo Press.

Sylva, K. (1994). School influences on children's development. *Journal of Child Psychology and Psychiatry, 35*(1), 135–70.

Tarnowski, S. M. & Murphy, V. B. (2003). Recruitment, retention, retraining, and revitalization among elementary music teachers in Wisconsin and Minnesota. *Update: Applications of Research in Music Education, 22*(1), 15–28.

Taylor, L. C., Hinton, I. D., & Wilson, M. N. (1995). Parental influences on academic performance in African-American students. *Journal of Child and Family Studies, 4*(3), 293–302.

Tschannen-Moran, M., & Woolfolk Hoy, A. (2002 April). *The influence of resources and support on teachers' efficacy beliefs.* A paper presented at the annual meeting of the American Educational Research Association, New Orleans.

Terman, L. M. & Oden, M. H. (1947). The gifted child grows up: Twenty-five years' follow-up of a superior group. In L. M. Terman (ed.), *Genetic studies of genius* (Vol. IV). Stanford, CA: Stanford University Press.

Thatcher, R., Walker, R., & Giudice, S. (1987). Human cerebral hemispheres develop at different rates and ages. *Science, 236*(4805), 1110–13.

Thompson, R. A. & Nelson, C. A. (2001). Developmental science and the media: Early brain development. *American Psychologist, 56*(1), (Jan.), 5–15.

Torrance, E. P., & Safter, H. T. (1990). *The incubation model of teaching.* Buffalo: Bearly Limited.

Tramo, M. J. (2001). Music of the hemisphere. *Science, 291*(5501), 54–56.

Trehub, S. E. (2000). Music and infants: Research findings and implications. In *Harmonic development: Music's impact to age three* (pp. 52–67). Pittsburgh: Pittsburgh Symphony.

Trehub, S. E. (2006). Infants as musical connoisseurs. In G. McPherson (ed.), *The child as musician* (pp. 33–49). Oxford: Oxford University Press.

Trehub, S., Bull, D., & Thorpe, L. (1984). Infants' perception of melodies: The role of melodic contour. *Child Development, 55*, 821–30.

Trevarthen, C. & Malloch, S. (2002a). Musicality and music before three: Human vitality and invention shared with pride. *Zero to Three, 23*, 10–18.

Trotter, R. J. (1987). Growth spurts mirror mental milestones: Cerebral hemisphere development. Research by Thatcher, R. W. *Psychology Today, 21*, 13.

Tse, M. M. Y., Chan, M. F., Benzie, I. F. F. (2005). The effect of music therapy on postoperative pain, heart rate, systolic blood pressures and analgesic use following nasal surgery. *Journal of Pain & Palliative Care Pharmacotherapy, 19*(3), 21–29.

Tyler, F. B., Rafferty, J. E., & Tyler, B. B. (1962). Relationships among motivations of parents and their children. *Journal of Genetic Psychology, 101*(1), 69–81.

Upitis, R., & Smithrim, K. (2001). *Learning through the arts, national assessment, a report on year one.* Kingston, ON: unpublished from Queens' University and the Royal Conservatory of Music.

Upitis, R., Smithrim, K., Patteson, A., & Meban, M. (2001). The effects of an enriched elementary arts education program on teacher development, artist practices, and student achievement: Baseline student achievement and teacher data from six Canadian sites. *International Journal of Education and the Arts, 2*(8).

U.S. War Department (1945). Music in reconditioning in ASF convalescent and general hospitals (TB Med. 187). Washington, DC: U.S. War Department.

Vaughn, K. (2000). Music and mathematics: Modest support for the oft-claimed relationship. *Journal of Aesthetic Education, 34*(3–4), 149–66.

Verny, T. (1981). *The secret.* New York: Dell Publishers.

Vygotsky, L. (1978). *Mind in society: The development of higher psychological processes* (M. Cole, et al., eds.). Cambridge, MA: Harvard University Press.

Warren, D. H. (1994). *Blindness and children: An individual differences approach.* New York: Cambridge University Press.

Weikart, P. S. (1987). *Round the circle.* Ypsilanti, MI: High/Scope Press.

Weinberger, N. M. (1998b). Brain, behavior, biology, and music: Some research findings and their implications for educational policy. *Arts Education Policy Review, 99*(3), 28–37.

Weinberger, N. M. (1998a). The music in our minds. *Educational Leadership, 56*, 36–40.

Weinberger, N. M. (1999b). Lessons of the music womb. *MUSICA Research Notes 6*(1) 1–5.

Weir, B. (1989). A research base for pre-kindergarten literacy programs. *Reading Teacher, 42*(7), 456–60.

Whitwell, D. (1997). *Music learning through performance.* Austin: Texas Music Educators Association.

Willingham, L. (2007). From the mouths of babes: What young children can show us about teaching and learning music—a personal reflection. In K. Smithrim & R. Upitis (eds.), *Listen to their voices: Research and practice in early childhood music.* Toronto, ON: Canadian Music Educators Association.

Winner, E. (1996a). *Gifted children: Myths and realities.* New York: Basic Books.

Winner, E. (1996b). The rage to master: The decisive role of talent in the visual arts. In K. A. Heller, F. J. Monks, & A. H. Passow (eds.), *International handbook of research and development of giftedness and talent* (pp. 253–81). New York: Pergamon Press.

Wood, E. (2004). *International Suzuki Association* (n.d.). Retrieved May 25, 2008, from http://www.internationalsuzuki.org/shinichisuzuki.htm

Woolfolk Hoy, A. & Burke-Spero, R. (2003). *Changes in teachers' feelings of efficacy during the early years of teaching: An exploratory study.* Unpublished manuscript, Ohio State University.

Young, S. (2003a). *Music with the under-fours.* London: Routledge Falmer.

About the Author

Maureen Harris, an educator and music professional, has dedicated twenty years to the education of the young child. She earned a master's of education at the University of Windsor and studied early childhood music with Dr. Edwin E. Gordon at Michigan State University. Harris is the creator of the early childhood music education programs Montessori Mozarts and Mozart and the Young Mind. She has conducted workshops and presented at conferences for MENC: The National Association for Music Education and the American Montessori Society in the United States; the Royal Conservatory of Music and the Music Therapy World Conference in Canada; and the Mathematical Bridges conference in Great Britain. Her publications include "Music and Math" in *Listen to Their Voices: Research and Practice in Early Childhood Music*, a text for early childhood educators published through the Canadian Music Educators Association; *Montessori Mozarts*, an instructional book for Montessori educators and parents; and this comprehensive early childhood music education book for music graduates and early childhood education graduates.